WHY BEING *Good* CAN BE **BAD** FOR YOU

HOW TO GET CLARITY, CONFIDENCE AND COURAGE TO STEP OUT OF STUCKNESS

KATE WITTEVEEN, PhD

First published by Ultimate World Publishing 2020
Copyright © 2020 Kate Witteveen

ISBN

Paperback - 978-1-922497-14-7
Ebook - 978-1-922497-15-4

Kate Witteveen has asserted her rights under the Copyright, Designs and Patents Act 1988 to be identified as the author of this work. The information in this book is based on the author's experiences and opinions. The publisher specifically disclaims responsibility for any adverse consequences which may result from use of the information contained herein. Permission to use information has been sought by the author. Any breaches will be rectified in further editions of the book.

All rights reserved. No part of this publication may be reproduced, stored in or introduced into a retrieval system, or transmitted in any form, or by any means (electronic, mechanical, photocopying, recording or otherwise) without the prior written permission of the author. Any person who does any unauthorised act in relation to this publication may be liable to criminal prosecution and civil claims for damages. Enquiries should be made through the publisher.

Cover design: Ultimate World Publishing
Layout and typesetting: Ultimate World Publishing
Editor: Hayley Ward
Cover image: pathdoc-Shutterstock.com

Ultimate World Publishing
Diamond Creek,
Victoria Australia 3089
www.writeabook.com.au

Testimonials

What a powerful, authentic, and raw book. Beautifully and professionally written. I feel that this book was written about me. If only I knew of Kate years ago, I could have saved so much time on these things she talks about. I'm going to have some in my yoga studio library for clients to see. This is a must read.

Trudy Vains,
Yoga Teacher and Birth Doula, Author of *Fused*

Kate has presented an inspiring journey of becoming unstuck from the pain of guilt, fear, frustration, and people pleasing. Kate is not only giving insight into the blocks, beliefs and behaviour patterns created as a result of perfectionism, but she depicts a wonderful and powerful journey through her own experience, that paved the way to personal growth, finding healthy boundaries, and returning to herself. Kate guides you through reconceptualising the way you think about yourself, from neutralising fear and releasing guilt to developing acceptance from within.

Shelley Maree Hunter, Disability and
Mental Health Worker, Author of *Face of Faith*

I loved Kate Witteveen's fresh and invigorating writing style. I was captivated by her ability to weave strategy, empirical research, and heart wrenchingly relatable storytelling into a beautiful book, sprinkled with wit and charm, that will leave the reader feeling confident about positive immediate action they can take in their own lives. A fantastic read!

Nikki Langman, International Speaker and Author of *How to be a BADASS*

Kate's journey and her powerful transformation into her authentic self was incredibly relatable for me, and I suspect many others who reach middle age and really start to wonder who they are. She is highly perceptive and writes with such empathy that I immediately felt connected to her story, and ready to sign up for her coaching! An important book for anyone who is ready to let go of pleasing others at the expense of their own satisfaction and fulfilment.

Fleur Hull, Career Strategist and Author

A phenomenal, refreshing and unique insight into the human psychology and character! Definitely a "must read" personal approach that is powerful, explicit and relatable to everyone!

Kate Witteveen has captured the essence of what it means to break free from our high expectations, judgements, criticism and demands, in order to create a magnificent life of courage, intention and alignment to core values and connection!

Taloa Walters, Author of *Spirit Freedom*, Co-owner of New Economic Evolution of the World/Evorich

Dedication

For Dad – who told me I could do anything.

For Mum – who never let me forget it.

For Michael – my only.

For Madelyn, Baxter, and Hugo – my everything.

Contents

Preface: A dodgy GPS as a metaphor for life ix
Introduction: Untenable xiii

**PART 1: CALCULATING THE COST –
UNCOMFORTABLE TRUTHS ABOUT BEING GOOD** 1
Chapter 1: Gotta Be Good 3
Chapter 2: Perfection*isnt* – Setting Yourself Up to Fail 7
Chapter 3: People Pleasing – When You Come Last 21
Chapter 4: Puritanical Perspective – No Shades of Grey 31

**PART 2: PONDERING THE POSSIBILITIES –
BREAKING UP WITH BEING GOOD** 39
Chapter 5: My Greatest Teacher 41
Chapter 6: Clarity – Maximising Discernment 49
Chapter 7: Confidence – Enhancing Certainty 63
Chapter 8: Courage – Harnessing Conviction 73

PART 3: STEPPING OUT OF STUCKNESS - ADOPTING AN ASTUTE MINDSET 79

Chapter 9: Align – Identifying Your Non-Negotiables and Deal-Breakers 83

Chapter 10: Set Intentions – Choose What You Want to BE and DO 91

Chapter 11: Thankfulness – Make Gratitude Your Superpower 99

Chapter 12: Undo – Undoing is Uncomfortable but Unavoidable 105

Chapter 13: Together – Your People Make Hard Times Easier and Good Times Better 119

Chapter 14: Elevate – Thank Yourself Later 129

Afterword 137
About the Author 141
Additional Resources and Opportunities 143

Preface

A dodgy GPS as a metaphor for life

On 16 March 2012, three Japanese tourists visiting Australia made headlines when they drove their Hyundai Getz hire car into the ocean whilst attempting to drive to North Stradbroke Island[1]. Unbeknown to them, North Stradbroke Island is only accessible by boat.

When these hapless travellers programmed their destination into their GPS device, the device did not take into account the 14 kilometres of water between the island and the mainland. Instead, it directed them straight into the tranquil waters of Moreton Bay.

Thankfully, none of the adventurous trio were harmed. Their hire car, however, was considerably worse off after its foray into the ocean. Apparently undeterred, the tourists expressed their intention to return to Australia, specifically to visit North Stradbroke Island (via ferry).

---

[1] Fujita, A. GPS Tracking Disaster: Japanese Tourists Drive Straight into the Pacific. www.abcnews.go.com

WHY BEING GOOD CAN BE BAD FOR YOU

When the story was broadcast, responses ranged from complete bewilderment (*"How can you drive into the ocean??"*) to outright mockery (*"Surely they knew their car couldn't swim??"*). In lunchrooms and at office water coolers throughout the country, many had a chuckle at the tourists' expense.

For me, though, there was something different. Reading that story gave me a visceral sensation that I associate with something I have dubbed "empathic mortification". That feeling arises when I feel desperately sorry for someone <u>and</u> recognise that their misfortune could easily be mine.

It feels exactly like mortification: a hot, burning sensation in my hands and a churning in my stomach, accompanied by a strong desire to disappear, at least until the situation is resolved (i.e., nobody is looking anymore). Alongside the mortification is a sense of relief. A "thank God that's not me," coupled with the recognition that it could have been.

For the record, I have never driven my car into the ocean. My car mishaps are limited to temporarily misplacing my car in the shopping centre carpark (albeit, on numerous occasions) and driving the wrong way up a one-way ramp at Pacific Fair Shopping Centre (ONCE, and under directions from my navigator!). However, I can understand how such a situation arose.

Quite simply, they were following the instructions that they were given, in good faith. They had identified that they didn't know how to get to North Stradbroke Island, and they trusted that the best way to get there was to follow the GPS device. At some point, they probably had doubts about the accuracy of the directions, but they didn't trust themselves enough to deviate from the prescribed course.

I understand their compliance completely. It is how I have lived most of my life, and it is why I wrote this book. Just like following

PREFACE

a GPS that has been incorrectly programmed, I have found myself following a path that wasn't correct for me. Trusting that others knew more than I did has gotten me into trouble on more than one occasion, and it is a habit I am actively trying to change.

Living according to what I <u>thought</u> was expected of me, or what a good girl, wife, mother, daughter, sister, friend, employee, would do, had me stuck on a path that was leading to my version of driving my car into the ocean. Except, instead of being knee-deep in water, I found myself burnt out, overwhelmed, and feeling like I was failing in every aspect of my life.

My journey from compulsive good girl to burnt-out academic didn't happen overnight, but it did happen. Whilst many factors contributed to my burnout, many of the decisions I made that led to that outcome stemmed from my desire to be good. The problem was that my definition of good was bad for me.

This book is about muting the external GPS that is no longer working for you. It is about finding the clarity, the confidence, and the courage to emphatically overrule that annoying voice telling you to go left when left leads to the ocean. And to be proud of yourself for doing so.

DISCLAIMER

Some names and identifying details have been changed to protect the privacy of individuals.

Introduction

Untenable

"You have a strong case, but it's going to cause a whole lot of trouble. I don't think that is what you want, is it?"

Those words were kryptonite to my client, Walter. They also sealed the fate of that chapter of his career. The person sitting across the table from him didn't know Walter very well, but they had found and exploited his greatest weakness with apparent ease. The depressing ambience of the soulless office in which he sat seemed apt for this conversation. He felt utterly defeated. It had taken a lot of courage to share that story, and he had done so for no quantifiable reason.

Of course, he didn't want to cause any trouble. Like me, Walter was a lifelong devotee of being good, and thus averse to causing trouble. To even contemplate causing trouble made him feel nauseous. He liked doing what was expected of him. Sadly, though, his unwillingness to cause trouble meant the career he had built over many years had become untenable.

WHY BEING GOOD CAN BE BAD FOR YOU

The trouble Walter was discouraged from causing was the type of trouble that needed to be caused. It was a version of the "good trouble" that Civil Rights leader John Lewis dedicated his life to causing. Good trouble that spoke out and stood up against injustice, unfairness, and inequality. In this case, the issues were workplace bullying and professional sabotage, which culminated in Walter seeking assistance from his organisation and being advised that taking action was not a feasible option.

Regrettably, Walter did not cause good trouble. Like many of us would have done in his situation, he complied with the advice he was given and shut up. And then he walked away from his career because the cost of staying was his health and his well-being. He had reached his pivotal point, and there was no way to stay.

When listening to Walter recounting that fateful conversation, I had a strong sense of déjà vu. Like Walter, I could recall a defining conversation where everything changed. My pivotal point may have been borne of different circumstances, but the theme was common: reaching a point at which you know you have no choice but to walk away from what is familiar. Recognising that you are confusing familiar with safe, when in fact your familiar is toxic.

Walter and I both experienced a significant burnout. We had a shared tendency to be exemplary organisational citizens, which unfortunately translated into being crappy stewards of our health and well-being. It can be devastating to realise that doing all the right things, ticking all the boxes, and saying yes to everything, has not delivered the outcome you desired.

Recognising that you have followed a script you thought was written for you personally, but was actually your interpretation of societal expectations, is confronting. However, the cost of continuing in that lane is hard to quantify. For Walter, and for me, it was burnout. For others, the costs have included relationship

INTRODUCTION

breakdowns (or staying in unhealthy relationships) and mental, emotional, and physical health challenges.

Being good was, in fact, bad for me; just as it has been for many of my clients, and perhaps for you too. In this book, I will share with you the challenges I have experienced, the lessons I have learned, and the gifts I have received on my journey back from burnout. That journey has required a significant amount of soul-searching, an unflinching look at how I created my own suffering, and a reconsideration of many beliefs I have held since childhood.

My burnout resulted in more than a career pivot. The impact was an existential crisis. Figuring out who I was when I wasn't an academic was painful. Even harder was acknowledging that the framework I was using to make important decisions was flawed. There was a misalignment between my intentions and my impact. Whilst I was always trying to be good and do my best, I was forgetting to be kind to myself in the process.

Thankfully, the outcome has been a life overhaul. But I'll be honest – it's still a work in progress. This is not my autobiography, but it does contain stories from my life. It isn't a chronology either. Rather, it is an amalgamation of stories that have contributed to my understanding of my over-reliance on being good to be accepted, and what assumptions I needed to question. Some of them are mine, others have been derived from the journeys of my clients.

I won't be presenting an empirically supported theory (although I will draw from some of those), and my conclusions are entirely lacking in statistical significance because they are based on anecdotal rather than empirical evidence. However, I have come to realise that there are different ways of knowing, that don't require a gold standard in research design. It is my hope that by sharing what (I think) I have figured out about the traps of striving to be good, I might save at least one of you some self-imposed suffering.

There are many ways in which being good can be bad for you. I have chosen three to focus on, because they are the recurring themes I have encountered in my own experience and with my clients. This is by no means an exhaustive list, and history is overflowing with heartbreaking examples when individuals and groups did as they were told rather than what was right. Those stories are beyond the scope of this book.

For the sake of simplicity, my premise is that being good can be bad for you because it contributes to faulty judgements that lead to negative outcomes, including:

1. Perfectionism (self-judgement);
2. People-pleasing (fear of judgement from others in close proximity); and
3. Puritanical perspective (fear of judgement from society at large).

In *Part 1 - Calculating the Cost - Uncomfortable Truths about Being Good*, I will share some of the ways in which these faulty judgements can cause negative impacts.

In *Part 2 - Pondering the Possibilities - Breaking up with Being Good*, I will outline the three attributes that will provide a foundation from which you can begin the process of de-emphasising the need to be good, in favour of other metrics that may serve you better.

Finally, in *Part 3 - Stepping out of Stuckness - Adopting an ASTUTE Mindset*, I will describe a framework that is helpful for getting beyond the constrictions of being good and embracing the opportunities that exist beyond that schema.

INTRODUCTION

Recognising that being good can be bad for you was hard for me, but it helped me redefine my criteria for success, and provided the impetus to improve my health and well-being. I hope that by relinquishing my need to be good, I can become better. Ironically, that requires lowering my expectations of myself, and cultivating the courage to be bad at new things. As I said: it's a work in progress.

If you can relate to the tendency to be good at the cost of being kind to yourself, you may be interested in the guide I have created to accompany this book: *"The Definitive Guide to Breaking Free from Being Good"*. It contains self-reflective exercises intended to help you examine your own beliefs and habits that may be contributing to your tendency to be good, and how those tendencies may be detrimental to you. It also contains exercises associated with the ASTUTE Transformation Framework, which is described in Part 3. You can download it for free here: www.katewitteveen.com.

Part 1

Calculating the Cost – Uncomfortable Truths About Being Good

Chapter 1

Gotta Be Good

"Then I came face to face with the realisation that disappointing people is the greatest fear of the nice girl."

Lynne Hybels, "Nice Girls Don't Change the World."

For as long as I can remember, I wanted to follow the rules. I have never liked to get things wrong or do things that would draw attention. The thought of breaking rules or causing trouble makes me uncomfortable. Equally, the thought of making mistakes in front of others has, historically, been a cause of extreme angst. In his research, social psychologist, Professor Matt Lieberman, has found that people would prefer to be hit by a car than to make a mistake in front of others[2]. I can totally relate to that finding.

---

[2] Lieberman, M.D. (2000). Intuition: A social cognitive neuroscience approach. Psychological Bulletin, 126(1), 109-137.

WHY BEING GOOD CAN BE BAD FOR YOU

I grew up in a small regional town where almost everybody knew each other. My father was the principal of the local Catholic primary school, so we were somewhat visible in the town. We were frequently reminded that we should not misbehave in public because it would reflect poorly on Dad. I took that warning to heart, and rarely got into trouble at school. However, on one memorable occasion, my Year 8 class, which had the dubious honour of being the most notorious class in our year level, received a class detention. We had to pick up rubbish for the first 15 minutes of our lunch break.

It is not an exaggeration to say mortification had me in its grip for the entire duration of that detention. As I picked up rubbish, I felt the searing burn of shame coursing through my body. I remember looking at the troublemakers in disgust and disbelief at how completely unaffected they were. I understand now that I felt shame because this punishment challenged the very essence of my identity. But at the time, I didn't have that insight. Instead, I had a strong desire to curl up somewhere and become invisible.

It wasn't about the rubbish or that the punishment cut into my lunch time. It also wasn't the injustice that I, along with many other innocents, were being punished for the actions of a few. It was the exposure, the visibility, and the intense scrutiny I felt during the detention. My self-conscious 13-year-old brain believed that everyone was looking at me and forming judgements about who I was. Getting into trouble cut to the core of my identity.

Decades later, I have compassion for my younger self. Whilst it is easy to dismiss this experience as a minor blip on an otherwise unblemished behavioural record, it was much more than that for me. Even though the punishment wasn't aimed at me as an individual, it usurped my need to be good, and it hurt more than it should have.

With the benefit of time, experience, reflection, and a willingness to look hard and unblinkingly at the content and origin of my core beliefs, I can see that the only judgements about my worth were being made by me. As Olin Miller once said, *"You probably wouldn't worry about what people think of you if you could know how seldom they do!"*

However, at that point in my life, anything which made me visible made me uncomfortable. Nobody else saw me differently because I was in a class detention. Only me. And that is one of the traps of the need to be good. It becomes part of your identity, and it is extremely confronting to have that aspect of your sense of self challenged.

This memory should not be one of my most vivid recollections from high school. Reflecting on the many notable events that occurred during that time, this is the odd one out. Rationally, this minor incident should not share the memory stage with big-ticket items like forming lifelong friendships and sharing experiences such as speech nights and school camps.

It doesn't justify the allocation of emotional and cognitive energy that goes into remembering something for decades. It doesn't deserve its place in my finite memory bank, where salience is at a premium. Holding onto it is costing me access to other things I would prefer to remember. Yet, there it is, prominent and unwavering in my high school narrative; vivid and evocative, reminding me how important it was to be good.

I deliberately chose this example to illustrate how being good can distort your perception of reality. By any account, getting a class detention is no big deal. It is an insignificant, almost laughable, deviation from being good. However, to me, at that stage of my life, it was monumental (and, clearly, memorable).

WHY BEING GOOD CAN BE BAD FOR YOU

That theme has continued throughout my life, and there have been other instances where a minor aberration has felt like a major disaster. Although I no longer shudder at the thought of that detention, I can still muster up the pang of self-consciousness when I think of more recent examples. Having recognised the traps of being overly attached to being good, I consider myself a recovering perfectionist. Like any lifelong habit, it takes some undoing.

Chapter 2

Perfection*isnt* – Setting Yourself Up to Fail

Perfectionist: *noun* = a person who refuses to accept any standard short of perfection.

Perfectionisnt: *noun* = a neologism (nonsense word) I created to account for the fact that striving for perfection is unrealistic and limiting, and often leads to feelings of inadequacy.

If you have ever responded to the customary job interview question, *"What is your greatest weakness?"* with, *"Well, I do tend to be a bit of a perfectionist,"* I have some bad news for you. Although there is some evidence to suggest that perfectionism is associated with higher levels of motivation and conscientiousness, there is a flipside.

Research has found that perfectionism is associated with a higher risk of stress, burnout, and anxiety. In addition, perfectionism doesn't necessarily translate to better performance. Ouch. Although a precise explanation for this finding remains elusive, one suggestion is that the amount of time spent perfecting a task impacts on other performance metrics, such as time management[3].

For me, the biggest trap of perfectionism isn't the time you waste trying to make sure everything is perfect. It's the internal narrative that accompanies the inevitable recognition that you fell short. Again. Perfectionism presents itself like a cantankerous, impossible-to-please supervisor in my head, overseeing everything I do and offering unhelpful feedback about the deficiencies only she can perceive. I have named that voice, "Naggy Nancy," and to be perfectly honest, she's quite a b*tch. If you are familiar with the TV show "Glee," Coach Sue Sylvester is Naggy Nancy personified.

One of the by-products of the Naggy Nancy phenomenon is Imposter Syndrome. A general definition of Imposter Syndrome is a feeling of not deserving your success. However, it can also feel like you are the least capable, qualified, confident, or competent person in the room/team/organisation. It can cause you to second guess yourself and live in fear of being found out as a fraud who doesn't know what they are doing. It can feel like you are wearing a mask, and you are afraid to let it slip, in case your authentic self is not enough. I believe Imposter Syndrome occurs when Naggy Nancy and her equivalents get too much airtime.

Interestingly, Imposter Syndrome causes highly capable and outwardly successful individuals to live in fear of being outed

---

[3] Swider, B., Harari, D., Breidenthal, A.P., and Steed, L.B. (2018). The pros and cons of perfectionism, according to research. *Harvard Business Review*. www.hbr.org/2018/12/.

as a phony. Although Imposter Syndrome is not an official diagnosis, it is a common experience, and it can be associated with negative psychological outcomes. Believing you are not worthy of your success, or that you are successful in spite of, rather than because of, your knowledge, skills, and abilities, is exhausting. You feel like you are being deceitful, when in fact you are not. This means you feel the burden of a lie that is not a lie.

Like all shame-inducing narratives, Imposter Syndrome cannot flourish under the glare of transparency. The best way to shift your Imposter Syndrome is to place it under the spotlight and see what it is actually made of. Although it takes courage, it is worthwhile to dare to question the validity of your Imposter Syndrome beliefs and see how they stack up under scrutiny. In my experience, the beliefs underpinning Imposter Syndrome rarely hold weight when they are evaluated objectively.

Over the years, my ability to discern whether or not to pay attention to Naggy Nancy has improved, but she has wreaked some havoc along the way. Her vantage point inside my consciousness means she knows my weaknesses, and she exploits them unapologetically. She is a master manipulator with an unparalleled capacity to make me doubt myself. There were times throughout my PhD journey where I felt as though I was simultaneously gaining a Masters in Imposter Syndrome. Along with questions about my research topic, I was extremely adept at asking Imposter Syndrome-inducing questions.

"Do you really think that is good enough?"

"Are you sure you should do that?"

"What if you've made a mistake? You probably have. No, I'm sure you have."

"What if that's not right?"

WHY BEING GOOD CAN BE BAD FOR YOU

"I don't think that is actually good enough."

"Look at what you haven't done properly."

"Everybody is going to look at you. They are looking right now."

"That's not the best way to do it. You should ask someone else."

And so on. Blah blah. Shut up, Naggy Nancy!

Asking my clients about the little voice inside their heads that shouts about the need for perfection has taught me some noteworthy things about Naggy Nancy.

1. She is definitely not an indication that I am going crazy. I am yet to come across someone who can relate to being a perfectionist who doesn't have an inner critic that sounds a lot like Nancy.

2. She is not even slightly original. Although we all pride ourselves on our uniqueness, I have identified that inner critics are remarkably lacking in creativity. They all appear to have an unsurpassed ability to cause fear and self-doubt and are adept at honing in on the most fundamental fear shared by most of humanity, namely: I am not enough.

Renowned psychoanalyst, Karen Horney (in case my brothers are reading this and giggling – it's pronounced Horn-eye), proposed a model of self-concept which included a construct known as the "tyranny of the should". My potentially sacrilegious oversimplification of Horney's model is thus:

Each individual has a belief about who they currently are ("real self") and who they could or should be ("ideal self"). The difference between those two concepts of self contributes to the development (or not) of neurosis. Those with a notable distance between their real and ideal selves are more likely to be neurotic and therefore motivated by the "tyranny of the should". This means that they consistently strive to meet unrealistic expectations or "shoulds" in order to decrease the discrepancy between the real and ideal selves.

For example:

> "He should be the utmost of honesty, generosity, considerateness, justice, dignity, courage, unselfishness. He should be the perfect lover, husband, teacher. He should be able to endure everything, should like everybody, should love his parents, his wife, his country; or, he should not be attached to anything or anybody, nothing should matter to him, he should never feel hurt, and he should always be serene and unruffled. He should always enjoy life; or, he should be above pleasure and enjoyment. He should be spontaneous; he should always control his feelings. He should know, understand, and foresee everything. He should be able to solve every problem of his own, or of others, in no time. He should be able to overcome every difficulty of his as soon as he sees it. He should never be tired or fall ill. He should always be able to find a job. He should be able to do things in one hour which can only be done in two or three hours[4]."

Sounds exhausting, doesn't it? I don't consider myself neurotic, and I don't think I am compelled by the tyranny of the should. However, a less extreme version of this idea that sits pretty comfortably within my personal experience of perfectionism is the "tyranny of the good". Although lacking any empirical support, I am comfortable that there is anecdotal evidence for this idea. The "tyranny of the good" is the compulsion to give Naggy Nancy credibility. In the hope of muting Naggy Nancy (and her counterparts), I am calling her out and naming her most common plays and how they impact me, and all my fellow recovering perfectionists. I think of these as the "traps of perfectionism".

---

[4] Horney, K. (1950). *Neurosis and Human Growth: The Struggle Toward Self-Realization*. New York: W. W. Norton & Company, Inc. (1991 edition), p. 65.

The traps of perfectionism

1. You focus on the imperfections

Collecting my PhD from the bookbinders was a momentous occasion. The shiny navy cover with gold lettering was smooth to the touch, and the 300 pages within that shiny cover represented almost six years of effort, self-doubt, persistence, and many sleepless nights trying to remember why I had thought doing a PhD was a good idea. Completing my PhD at the same time as starting my family and working fulltime was no small undertaking, and I was proud of myself for getting it across the line. I remember driving to the bookbinders with a sense of delicious anticipation of the moment I would finally hold that weighty tome with my name on the front in my hands. That was the moment I knew it would become real. I had earned the right to doff my floppy hat and move on with my life.

However, Naggy Nancy, perfectionist-in-residence, wasn't satisfied. Along with being a master manipulator, one of her superpowers is being a massive killjoy. Celebrating achievements is one of her pet peeves, and she always finds a way to gatecrash and ruin those parties. Among the many reasons for her dissatisfaction with the final product, was the observation that in the printing of the document, one of the tables had spread across two pages.

This is undoubtedly a formatting fail, and one that has niggled me for many years. It should not neutralise the sense of achievement of actually completing a PhD, but it did. My discomfort with this imperfection was so substantial that I had to actively stop myself from commenting on it when people congratulated me on completing my PhD. Can you imagine the awkwardness?

"Hey, congrats on finishing your PhD. That's a great achievement!"

"Thanks, but it's not that big a deal. One of the tables goes across two pages, so it's kind of a stuff up, really."

Cringey, isn't it?

As this story suggests, one of the superpowers of the perfectionist is to find a way to minimise, trivialise or criticise their accomplishments. So, if you compliment a perfectionist, be prepared for that compliment to be rebutted rather than received. If you are a perfectionist, pay attention the next time you are given a compliment. Can you accept and receive it, or do you feel the need to put a caveat around it? "Thanks, but [insert self-deprecating limitation here]..."

This difficulty in accepting compliments is not, in my understanding, false modesty or attention-seeking. For me, at least, it is about honesty. Because I focus on the imperfections, I feel bound to point them out to others. Authenticity is one of my core values, so I want to make sure that any praise I receive is based on a full understanding of the actual product. I don't want to mislead people into thinking that something I have done is more impressive than it is. The difference is, I now catch myself doing it much sooner than I used to. This early catch gives me options: do I focus on the imperfections, or do I celebrate the rest?

I do seem to be a slow learner in this regard. I have had many opportunities to refine this tendency, but I am still working on it. In my life as an academic, I had the perfect opportunity to practise receiving feedback. As was standard practice, I would receive teaching evaluations at the end of each semester. Typically, my reports were extremely positive, and I appreciated the constructive comments from my students.

However, I didn't focus on them, and, sadly, I can't really remember them. I would skim-read past those comments associated with the 5-star ratings, and hone in on the small minority of low ratings and negative comments. They hurt like hell but were magnetic in drawing my attention.

Often those comments were purely based on personal preference of the student who, for whatever reason, didn't like my teaching style (or my refusal to give complete notes to students, based on my firm belief that to do so was a pedagogical disservice to students). Others were obviously malicious, and not based on my teaching at all. Some of the more memorable ones related to my dress sense and the fact that the student was quite convinced they had diagnosed me with social anxiety.

The irony of the social anxiety comment was that it was made in an evaluation of the unit, "Psychological Disorders". The first lecture in that unit was about ethics and diagnosis, and I had gone to great lengths to emphasise how important it was NOT to label or diagnose without following proper protocols, and the fact that completing an undergraduate course did not qualify them as diagnosticians. The other troubling feature of that comment was it demonstrated a complete lack of understanding of the symptoms of social anxiety. So, on reflection, perhaps the negative rating was justified in the sense that I had apparently taught them nothing!

I could rationalise that those comments didn't actually reflect my teaching ability, but that did not negate their capacity to drown out the positive comments. Naggy Nancy was in her element. She would helpfully remind me of all the nasty things the students had said. She neglected to acknowledge the fact that they either weren't true or were beyond the scope of what was reasonable to report in a teaching evaluation.

Those negative comments hurt and made it difficult to even acknowledge, let alone be proud of the positive comments, which significantly and substantially outnumbered and outweighed the negative ones. This overemphasis of the negative at the expense of the positive is also a contributing factor to one of the other traps of perfectionism – fear of trying and failing.

2. You are afraid of trying new things

"I'm afraid that if I try that I won't be good at it."

Every Perfectionist Ever

Without exception, my clients are highly accomplished, intelligent, and motivated individuals. Although their reasons for working with me differ, typically they share a desire to explore what else is possible for them. They feel a bit stuck in their current circumstances and want some support to identify other options. Many of them also share a tendency towards perfectionism, and this translates to a fear of doing new things. Like me, their desire to be good and not make a fool of themselves is a barrier to exploring new opportunities.

Ironically, it is this fear of failure that is most likely keeping them stuck. When you study the stories of the most successful people throughout history, one of the most prominent characteristics they have in common is a willingness to try, fail, and try again. The examples of genuine trailblazers demonstrating their willingness to fail are endless. And I am not talking about failing a few times before getting it right. It is reported that Thomas Edison created almost 10,000 unsuccessful prototypes before he invented the lightbulb.

Apart from that number being genuinely staggering, it says something about persistence, stamina, and self-belief. It also says a lot about a lack of perfectionism. Edison can't possibly have thought all 10,000 of his prototypes were great. However, it is hard to say whether or not he would have invented the lightbulb if he had been unwilling to experiment with even one of those failed prototypes. When we allow our fear of getting it wrong to stop us from having a go, it is impossible to know what we could be missing.

It is essential that we reconceptualise failure as learning opportunities, and this is most pertinent to the perfectionists. When we cling to the need to be good at things, we deprive ourselves of many opportunities to learn and grow. Michael Jordan is recognised as being one of the greatest basketball players of all time. He is also credited with saying, *"I've failed over and over again in my life. And that is why I succeed."* According to Jordan, he didn't succeed in spite of his failures, but because of them.

That is not to say Jordan and others who are experts don't aim for perfection. Of course they do. But there is a difference between committing to the refinement of your craft through deep, dedicated practice, and expecting yourself to be good at everything. The process of mastery includes, and actually requires, failure. It is from failure that we gather data that allows us to refine our attempts and do better next time. Doing something badly can provide critical information about what needs to change in order to do it well.

On his popular podcast, "Finding Mastery," sport and performance psychologist, Dr Michael Gervais routinely asks his guests for their definition of mastery. As the guests are, without exception, leaders in their fields, the definitions are typically well-considered, articulate, and often based on empirical findings. One of my favourite definitions was shared by former surfing world champion, Mick Fanning. For Fanning, the definition of mastery is: *"Trial and error."* Whether it was intentional or not, this definition, as brief and as simple as it is, captures much of what an established body of research has found. In order to succeed, we have to be willing to fail.

This appreciation for the power of failure is in stark contrast to the quote I shared at the beginning of this section. Although not specifically attributed to anyone in particular, that theme is one I have heard (and said) more times than I can count. Perfectionists see the possibility of failing as a reason not to try. This is self-defeating, and one of the traps of perfectionism that keeps people stuck. It also aligns seamlessly with the next trap of perfectionism: unrealistic expectations.

3. You place unrealistic expectations on yourself, and then judge yourself harshly when you don't meet them

Returning to work fulltime after my maternity leave with my third child, Hugo, signalled the beginning of one of the most challenging periods of my life. One of my most vivid memories from this time was the Mother's Day party at Hugo's daycare when he was two years old. He was attending childcare five days per week and, although he coped well, I struggled with guilt about how much time he spent there.

Attending special events at school and daycare has always been important to me, and I usually managed to find a way to make that happen, even if I was answering emails whilst cheering at the sports carnival. Whether the kids appreciated it or not, it was a salve against my mother guilt, and I was committed to showing up as often as I could.

However, on this occasion, I wasn't able to perform my mummy/employee juggling act. I was working on a major project which involved stakeholders from the upper echelons of the university. A meeting was scheduled for the same time as the daycare party, and I had no discretion to change it or miss it. When I finally made it to daycare, with a fake smile plastered on my face, ready to pretend to be enthusiastic about the party I knew I was unforgivably late for, the party was over. Hugo was crestfallen because we had missed the party, and I was devastated because I had failed him.

As I apologised profusely to Hugo for missing the party, I explained that I had tried really hard to get there, but I had to be at work. His bottom lip quivered, and tears filled his eyes. He took a moment to consider my explanation, and then he passed his judgement, with a sense of finality and decisiveness worthy of a High Court Justice: "Too much work, Mummy."

Indeed, it was. Although I hadn't done anything wrong, I felt so much guilt. It was too much work if I was simultaneously holding myself to an unattainable standard of parenting. My obligation to attend that meeting was not in question, and I had not chosen to miss the party. I had simply created unrealistic expectations for myself that I could be and do everything for everyone, and that there wouldn't be a cost.

The cost to Hugo was a temporary disappointment. He doesn't even seem to remember it. I recently asked him if he remembered the Mother's Day party at daycare, and he happily regaled the details of one of the parties from a different year, that I did attend. The cost to me was much greater and longer-lasting, and it stemmed almost entirely from my own unrealistic expectations.

There is no rule that says the only way to be a good parent is to attend every function. There is not even a rule that says you can't occasionally disappoint your children. In fact, it's probably helpful if you do, as it gives them the opportunity to develop an understanding that disappointment is inevitable. However, the amount of mother guilt and self-recrimination I carried about that party was crushing. Even talking about it years later was enough to reduce me to tears. But the reality was, there was no actual harm done. My self-judgement and condemnation were entirely unnecessary, and good examples of this trap of perfectionism.

Breaking up with perfectionism

If I have convinced you that perfectionism is more like perfectionisnt, welcome to the quest of the recovering perfectionist. Like any unwanted behavioural pattern, recognising the traps of perfectionism and the negative impact they can have is a great first step in breaking the grip of perfectionism. Unfortunately, that Naggy Nancy is a persistent creature, and shutting her up isn't a once-and-done venture. However, if you think of perfectionism as a habit, rather than a characteristic, you create the possibility that it is something you can choose, or not.

Chapter 3

People Pleasing – When You Come Last

"I can't tell you the key to success, but the key to failure is trying to please everyone."

Ed Sheeran

The need to be good can also be associated with the tendency to have trouble saying, "No". Not wanting to cause upset or offence, those who want to be good can easily fall into the trap of people pleasing. Like perfectionism, at first glance, people pleasing may not appear problematic. It can be perceived in many positive ways, such as being agreeable, helpful, friendly, a team player, a real asset to the organisation. Great! These are undoubtedly wonderful attributes to have, and we all want to be around people like that.

However, like perfectionism, there is a dark side to people pleasing. Habitual people pleasers may find themselves becoming frustrated or resentful that they are always the "go to" whenever somebody wants something. They can also find themselves so busy doing things for everyone else that they neglect to get their own stuff done. Or worse, they run themselves ragged to fit it all in, and their health suffers as a result.

Although research shows that if you want something done, you should give it to a busy woman (preferably a working mother, according to this study[5]), everyone has their limit. The people pleasers are just less likely to acknowledge when they have reached theirs. They are vulnerable to being taken advantage of, and this can have disastrous consequences.

The traps of people pleasing

1. You say "Yes" too often

One of the first exercises I get new coaching clients to complete is the Aspirations Exercise. I was introduced to this exercise during my Conversational Intelligence® training, and I loved it. The idea is to generate as many aspirations for life as possible (with 100 being the goal, but as many as you can is fine). Aspirations are different from goals in the sense that they are loftier, and there is no requirement that they seem feasible or achievable in the current moment. The beauty of this exercise is that it encourages creativity and exploration, and almost everyone who does it discovers something they didn't realise they wanted to do.

When I completed the Aspirations Exercise, I included many lofty and exciting aspirations. However, one of the least lofty and

---

[5] Krapf, M., Ursprung, H.W., & Zimmermann, C. (2014). *Parenthood and productivity of highly skilled labor: Evidence from the Groves of Academe*. Research Division, Federal Reserve Bank of St Louis. doi.org/10.20955/wp.2014.001

most unexciting was the one that remains the most salient. That aspiration was: *"Say yes when I mean yes, and say no when I mean no."* Granted, this is dull and not very inspirational, but for me, it is aspirational. It is also life-enhancing when I implement it.

Like many who like to be good, I can struggle to set limits, and saying "No" is difficult to do. I don't want to let anyone down, and I like to contribute, so I am easy fodder for door-to-door salespeople. The worst part is not the number of times I have been sucked in to changing my electricity provider (not because of the good deal, but because the salesperson asked so nicely!), but the self-recrimination that accompanies it.

When it became possible to list your home phone number on the "Do not disturb" register, I was weak with relief. It meant I was spared the quandary of not wanting to let down the nice salesperson on the end of the phone whose call was unsolicited and whose product I neither wanted nor needed. Intellectually, I knew I was under no obligation, but I found myself saying, "Yes" over and over again.

If I struggle to say no to strangers (albeit friendly ones), you can imagine how hard it is to say no to people I know. I am so easily guilted into doing things, especially for a good cause, that I have had to develop strategies to avoid becoming a fulltime volunteer. One of those strategies was to volunteer my husband instead. It seemed like a reasonable approach, but he didn't really appreciate it.

In all seriousness, not being able to say "No" can cause a major drain on resources, including time, energy, and emotion. The amazing thing is, I am yet to come across a terrible situation that arose from a reasonable person saying "No," especially if it is to an unreasonable request. The more detrimental outcomes are associated with the excessive "Yes," which can lead to resentment and overwhelm.

2. You say "No" too often

The other part of my aspiration was to say, "Yes when I mean yes". This is to overcome my tendency of saying "no" because I think it is what others want to hear, or because that is what a good girl would say. There have been many occasions when an opportunity has been presented, and I have said no too quickly. I have talked myself out of it before I had a chance to really consider it. The reasons I create for saying no are typically very rational, logical, and defensible, and entirely derived from my intellect. One of the hazards of using a good girl schema as a decision-making framework can be that you evaluate options against criteria such as "sensible" rather than "fun".

One of my clients described this tendency eloquently when she shared with me a newly acquired passion for snow skiing, that she very nearly missed altogether. Growing up in a major international city, she had little exposure to extreme sports, and outdoor adventures occurred only in her imagination.

When her friends invited her to join them on a skiing holiday, she accepted the invitation with some reluctance. Her total lack of experience in any extreme sports, and her intense fear of trying new things, combined to create an intensely negative visceral response. She was adamant that there was no way she was getting on those skis. In fact, she probably wouldn't even go near the slopes.

However, when the time came, she was inextricably drawn to the mountain. Seeing the joy in her friends' faces as they sped down the slopes was compelling. Despite her initial response being "no" and her determined refusal to even consider the possibility, she found herself lacing up her clunky ski boots and locking them into her first set of skis. After her first lesson, she was hooked. To her tremendous surprise, she was a natural.

The movements felt instinctive, and the freedom and exhilaration she felt whizzing down the mountain were captivating. She had never felt more alive, or more like herself, and she could so easily have missed it. Her habit of saying no too often could have deprived her of that experience. Finding her passion for skiing has made a profound impact on her life and opened up possibilities that she had previously never considered.

This is not to say that we need to say yes to everything and take up every opportunity that presents itself. However, it is worth pausing to notice: when you say no to something, is it an automatic or a considered response? What are the criteria you are using to decide? Giving yourself the gift of asking "why not" could be the key to finding your passion. Or, at the very least, having a great time!

3. You put up with things you shouldn't

Remember my client, Walter, who was talked out of making good trouble? As you may have guessed, Walter was the epitome of a people pleaser. He was a valued member of a large organisation, and he had a reputation as someone who could be counted on to get things done. Walter didn't engage in office politics and was well-liked throughout the organisation. Except for a brief secondment to another agency, he had worked at his organisation for several years, and was one of the longest-serving members of his team. He possessed organisational wisdom that can only be accrued over an extended timeframe, and he was generous in sharing his knowledge and expertise with others.

When Walter was presented with an opportunity to join an extraordinary project team, he had his reservations. The project was outside of his immediate area of expertise, but he undoubtedly possessed knowledge and skills that would add value. Also, the project had the potential to enhance his career trajectory. There were many logical reasons to join the project. Walter's challenge was that something felt off.

The project lead was brought in as an external consultant, and there were early signs of politicking that didn't sit well with Walter. However, Walter wasn't in the habit of listening to his intuition. He was more of an intellect kind of guy. Also, he didn't want to disappoint anyone, and, as the accomplished people pleaser that he was, he decided to set aside his reservations and join the team.

Walter's intuition had been correct, and his time on the project team was mired with white-anting and sabotage. Almost immediately, it became evident that the external consultant had an agenda that did not align with Walter's understanding of the purpose of the project. Whilst Walter had joined the project because he believed it would benefit his organisation and boost the career of his teammates and himself, the external consultant exploited his role with acts of self-aggrandisement and nepotism.

After Walter's initial surprise when it became evident that the project lead had used his influence to appoint a blatantly unqualified project officer, he did what he always did. He assumed that he was wrong, and the project officer was more qualified than she appeared. What Walter came to realise was that the project officer's claim to the position was not in her curriculum vitae; it was in her status as the project lead's mistress.

Nepotism aside, Walter persisted with the project. He worked hard, contributed as much as he could, and stayed away from the politics to the greatest extent possible. There was a clear disparity with regard to how team members were valued, but Walter tried not to get too despondent. Despite feeling undermined and undervalued, he continued to contribute. He tried to ignore the project officer's ineptitude and did what he was asked.

However, even Walter the people pleaser had his limits. In a team meeting where the project officer presented a proposal that was horrifyingly lacking in merit, Walter spoke up. With his typically non-combative style, Walter asked some questions to ensure he wasn't misunderstanding the proposal. The project officer became defensive, then aggressive, and then threw a tantrum and stormed out of the meeting. Although Walter had not intended to cause any upset, the proposal was so flawed he believed he owed it to his organisation to identify its lack of feasibility.

Walter's experience in the project team deteriorated. Whereas before he had been largely overlooked, he was now targeted by the project lead. It was clear that he was being punished, and his place on the project team was irrevocably altered the moment he had dared to question the project officer. Despite his best efforts to manage the situation, it became unbearable. A clear pattern of bullying emerged, with both the project lead and the project officer constantly sabotaging Walter.

This prolonged attack impacted Walter's health and well-being. Ultimately, he experienced a significant burnout, which made it difficult for him to continue in the team. When he became aware of other examples of misconduct on the part of the project lead, he knew he could no longer participate in the project team. The misconduct was so significant that it had both ethical and legal implications, so Walter reported it to his organisation. He took his role as an organisational citizen seriously and knew that he was required to report breaches of the Code of Conduct.

Despite knowing that stepping down from that project team had the potential to jeopardise his career, Walter knew he had to do it. The cost of staying was his health, and that was a cost he wasn't willing to pay. However, Walter's people pleasing wasn't finished with him yet. It had kept him stuck in a toxic project team, and then it kept him quiet.

As the organisation's representative pointed out the trouble his allegations would cause, Walter complied with the request to pretend it didn't happen. He wasn't forbidden from proceeding with his claim. He didn't need to be. He just needed to be reminded about what a good guy he was, and how much he didn't cause conflict or a fuss, and he was muted.

Breaking up with people pleasing

Whether you recognise yourself as saying yes too often, no too often, or putting up with things you shouldn't, the costs of people pleasing can be significant. You may not be a sucker for a telemarketer like I am, but perhaps the benefit of saying no more often resonates with you. Equally, you may not feel as though you have deprived yourself of the opportunity to find your great passion, but you may recall times when you haven't given yourself the gift of spontaneity or fun, because it wasn't a "good" idea. I hope you have never found yourself in a toxic situation like Walter, where you put up with bullying because you were uncomfortable speaking out. But perhaps you have, and you paid the price.

If any or all of these tendencies are familiar, I encourage you to consider the benefits of breaking up with people pleasing. This doesn't mean becoming self-absorbed or neglecting your responsibilities in favour of fun and frivolity. It also doesn't mean you can't do things to please others because you want to.

What it means is that you don't operate from a position of fear of what others will think if you are true to yourself. Rather than worrying about what people will think, ask yourself what aligns most strongly with your core values and beliefs. We will consider this in more detail In Part 3, as part of the ASTUTE Framework. For now, I encourage you to give yourself permission to make decisions based on moving towards situations that bring you joy, rather than moving away from fear of judgement.

Chapter 4

Puritanical Perspective – No Shades of Grey

"If your compassion does not include yourself, it's incomplete."

Jack Kornfield

Puritanical: *adjective* = of, or relating to, or characterised by a rigid morality.

The incessant need to be good can contribute to a rigid view of the world: things are either good or bad. This dichotomous thinking style is representative of a puritanical viewpoint. In this context, I am not referring to any specific moral or religious beliefs. It is more a recognition that clinging to the need to be good can result in harsh self-appraisals, and an unwarranted fear of judgement from others. This puritanical perspective is in direct contrast to self-compassion. Rather than accepting that we will inevitably make mistakes or poor choices, the puritanical perspective insists on complete adherence to absolute standards, and the self-recrimination that accompanies any breach can be suffocating.

When I was in primary school, I loved competing in school sporting events. As mentioned, my dad was the school principal, and all of my memories of swimming and athletics carnivals involve his cringeworthy commentary via a megaphone. He was a proud and vocal supporter and always let the crowd know when one of his kids was in the race. Although he was extremely professional and never gave me special treatment at school, for a few moments on sports day when I was competing, he put all pretence of objectivity aside and became a proud parent, rather than the principal.

At high school, I discovered that it wasn't cool to participate in sporting events. Competing was optional, and most people opted out. This created a dilemma for me. I wanted to fit in and be like my friends. I also wanted to compete. My family are quite competitive, but it has also been ingrained in us that it is important to participate and do your bit for your team.

In Year 8, I opted out of the swimming carnival and compromised for the athletics carnival. I agreed to participate in the 4 x 100m relay team. It was a good compromise. It was fun (and socially acceptable!) to be part of a team, but I wasn't overdoing it on the unwritten code of "trying too hard" that all of my peers seemed to have subscribed to. I had missed the memo but got the gist.

In Year 9, I took a chance and competed in two races at the swimming carnival. Again, nothing too showy. Just enough to do my bit for my team, whilst maintaining my allegiance to the unwritten Code of Cool. When it came to the athletics carnival, I faced a dilemma. Participation was really low. Nobody wanted to do the 1500m. Again, my family's emphasis on doing your bit for the team niggled at me, so I agreed to nominate for that event. Just to get a point for my team. Not to do anything silly like try to win or anything.

On the day of the athletics carnival, I felt the scratchiness of uncertainty and indecision. The visibility of being one of the few kids who actually cared about doing well felt uncomfortable, but the thought of not even trying felt disloyal to my family. Memories of my dad's proud face beaming at me whenever I crossed the finish line in my primary school carnivals floated around in the periphery of my awareness. Right up until the starting gun, I didn't know what I was going to do. I hadn't really trained for the event, but I knew I could run. With a bit of effort, I could probably do well.

With 14-year-old logic, I decided that fitting in with my peers was more important. I brushed aside my recollections of Dad's proud race commentary and reminded myself that this carnival was completely inconsequential. I reasoned with myself that nobody in my family even cared about this race. I had expressly forbidden my mum from attending the carnival, and it didn't occur to me that Dad would even remember it was on. He was so busy with his work, the high school sports carnival would be well outside his focus. Or so I thought.

When the starter's gun went off, a few eager competitors took off at a run, but I stayed at the back of the pack with the group that was meandering around the oval. What we were trying to prove is beyond me, but I think it was some kind of "too cool for this" message. To whom and for what reason, I don't really understand. I just knew that I didn't want to stand out or bring attention to myself as a try-hard, so I was sticking with the majority. There was safety in numbers, and that meant thumbing our noses at the spirit and intention of the carnival and walking the four laps of the oval to complete the 1500m.

After the first lap of walking, I looked up towards the school, and my breath caught in my throat. My dad's unmistakable

194cm frame silhouette was there, watching me be an idiot. I don't know how he knew when my race was on. There was no internet at this time, so he didn't have the luxury of a friendly reminder via TeamApp. We hadn't even talked about the carnival, and Dad had left for school early that day, so the red hair spray and zinc cream I was wearing in solidarity with my team hadn't tipped him off. But there he was. Watching me walking. And my shame was immense.

As soon as I saw him, my instincts kicked in, and I started to run. I couldn't bear the thought of him giving up time in his busy day to watch me be a brat, proving some ridiculous teenage point that made no sense, even to me. I had given up an entire lap of the oval lead, but as soon as I started running, I made up ground. By the end of the race, I had come in second. I took no pride in my second place ribbon. I felt only shame and embarrassment that my dad had come to cheer me on, and I had given him nothing to cheer about.

There were no recriminations about that race from Dad. In fact, I don't recall ever discussing it with him. At the time, I was too embarrassed. Apart from a mumbled, "Thanks for coming" at the dinner table that night, the race was not discussed. I assumed we would debrief it at some stage, but as it turned out, there wouldn't be much of an opportunity. Less than two months later, he would die unexpectedly from the heart condition we knew he had, but thought was under control.

The shock and horror of that loss cannot be adequately captured in words. The blessing that he died peacefully and pain-free is of some comfort now, as I have seen the horror of watching loved ones diminish over time from cancer. However, at that age, having never experienced suffering on that level, losing him so suddenly felt like the cruellest blow possible. I am proud of my mum, myself, and my brothers that none of us became the statistics we could have become as a result of that loss. However, the absence of a father, particularly one who was as involved and as present as ours, has lifelong ramifications.

I have discovered that you re-experience that loss in a new way with each new life stage. That is not to say that I am stuck in grief. But I have lost my dad in many ways and on many occasions, as I have journeyed through major milestones, and insignificant events alike, wishing he were here with us. I know how much he would have treasured all of his grandchildren, and the ache of knowing they all miss out on having him in their lives is truly heartbreaking.

Losing Dad at that stage of life also meant that I didn't get to ask him questions as I navigated my path through adolescence to adulthood. And I didn't get to ask him what that race meant to him. So I created a meaning, and in line with a puritanical perspective, I was harsh on myself. There was no compassion for the dilemma my 14-year-old self experienced: of being caught between what my friends were doing and what my family had taught me to do. The internal narrative I constructed about that race was immersed in shame. I could not allow myself to forget that the last time my dad watched me compete in something, I gave it a half-assed effort.

The memory of that day and the shame I felt about that race became a driving force in my life. I didn't realise it until recently, but it seems as though many of my decisions, even as an adult, have been based on my desire to never feel that shame again. And to make my dad proud of me. Of course, under different circumstances, that race would have been entirely forgettable. No big deal. It was the fact that it was the last time my dad watched me compete that gave it such significance. What started as an innocuous decision to fit in with the crowd became a defining moment in my life.

My judgement of myself about that race was formed from a puritanical perspective. I had created a firm dichotomy: make your parents proud or you should be totally ashamed. That dichotomy didn't take into account all the possible interpretations of the event. After carrying the burden of self-imposed shame about that race for 26 years, I recently worked up the courage to ask my mum if Dad had ever talked to her about that day. She said that he had. Given the volume and intensity of the shame and blame I had placed upon myself about that day, I was afraid to know what he said, but I asked her anyway. Expecting to hear how ashamed he was of me, I couldn't believe it when she said, *"He was impressed."*

What?? I thought I had misheard, or Mum had misunderstood. So, I clarified. I was talking about the day when I walked the first lap of the 1500m and only started running when I saw him standing there. Yes, Mum confirmed. That's what she was talking about also. *"He was impressed that you could give a lap headstart and still finish second."* I had difficulty processing, and then believing, what I was hearing. This empowering alternative interpretation of that race was perspective-shifting and life-altering for me. I could not believe I had never considered the possibility that he wasn't as ashamed of me as I was of myself.

But, upon reflection, and from the perspective of being a parent, it made total sense. My dad, ever the competitive spirit, was impressed that I could still get a place after being such a jerk. He loved a good podium finish, and clearly, this was no exception. Also true to form, he hadn't focused on the jerk bit, just the bit where I actually put in some effort. He hadn't made a big deal about it because he had understood. He also knew me well enough to know that I wouldn't put myself in that position again. Like him, I felt uncomfortable knowing I hadn't really tried, and I'm sure he knew I would learn from that experience and do better next time.

PURITANICAL PERSPECTIVE - NO SHADES OF GREY

The benefits of re-experiencing that event through a different lens are immeasurable. Giving my 14-year-old self the gift of compassion and understanding, and the recognition that wanting to fit in with my friends didn't make me a bad person, eradicated the shame almost instantaneously. It also highlighted how important it is to evaluate when, how and where our core beliefs are formed, and if they need to be re-examined. I had formed a core belief as a 14-year-old with a broken heart, and I had allowed that core belief to remain unchallenged for decades. The unquestioned puritanical framework of "all or nothing" resulted in self-flagellation and remorse that was unkind and unnecessary.

However, there is a gift in every lesson, and I have to acknowledge that, although I have punished myself unnecessarily, I have also derived positive motivation from that day. My faulty beliefs about the importance of that event provided fuel that kept me pushing towards goals that felt hard and beyond reach. It was once suggested to me that one of the reasons I have kept striving to do new things throughout my life is because I am trying to make my dad proud. Although he can never tell me that I've done enough, now that I have moved beyond my puritanical perspective of that event, I can stop trying to make up for the shame I thought I caused him on that dusty oval in 1994. The liberation from that shame is something precious to behold.

Part 2

Pondering the Possibilities – Breaking Up With Being Good

Chapter 5

My Greatest Teacher

"It is never too late to be what you might have been."

Mary Anne Evans

My youngest son, Hugo, is one of my greatest teachers. His personality is big, loud, gregarious, curious, and energetic. He loves people and gets upset when I don't invite the mailman in for a cup of tea when he is delivering packages. He also hates rules. Despises them. On principle. He is openly and unapologetically intolerant of rules, and how this came about is as much of a mystery to me as the fact that my daughter can sing. Both of these realities defy my expectations of how my genetic material should be expressing itself in my children.

A good example of Hugo's dislike of rules as a matter of principle is his persistent refusal to keep to the left of the path when he is riding his scooter. I have explained to him many times that it is a road rule (as opposed to a "Mum" rule), and it is a rule that we follow to keep everyone safe on the path. Hugo is unconvinced. He counters that he likes the middle of the path, he can see if someone is coming, and he thinks the rule is stupid. At the age of five, he can articulate a fairly compelling argument. You could argue that he over-relies on a straw man argument, but I give him credit for the strength of his convictions.

His distaste for rules is perplexing to me. As a lifelong rule abider, it has never occurred to me to question the rules like Hugo does. Each time he encounters a new rule, his default position is to test the parameters of that rule. He wants to know how far he can go beyond the rule before there is a consequence. More importantly, he wants to know if the consequence is even worth factoring into his decision about whether or not to stay within the parameters of the rule.

In reality, the presence of a consequence is typically not enough to encourage his compliance. He just likes to know what it is, and then he can decide if he wants to comply. Often he doesn't. The consequence is accepted as part of the deal. He will break the rule, and he will wear the consequence. No big deal. To him, at least.

In my defence, Hugo is probably more baffling to me because my older kids set me up with a false sense of confidence regarding the heritability of rule-following preferences. Baxter, in particular, loves rules. He thrives when he knows what they are and how to follow them. He even goes as far as asking me why other people break the rules. In his mind, rules are there for a reason. Why would you even want to break them? In these conversations, I have often shared his consternation.

Maddi falls somewhere in between. She doesn't inherently despise rules like Hugo, but she is also open to the possibility of discarding or ignoring them when they aren't to her liking.

Her aversion is not to the rules, but to the consequences. She vividly remembers getting into trouble once when she was in Year 1. That was enough for her. The thought of being elevated from the orange (warning) dot to the red (consequence) dot on the classroom whiteboard was enough to get her back to obedience. So, overall, my parenting schema was initially forged with rule-followers. Parenting Hugo has been an entirely different experience, and I have felt like a newbie parent all over again.

Hugo started school this year. Although his disdain for rules was common knowledge in our family, somehow it hadn't occurred to me that this would extend to school rules. On reflection, this was an oversight. I should have predicted that Hugo would take some time to adapt to the highly structured environment of school, where there are more rules than he has encountered in his life thus far.

Hugo's first semester report card confirmed what we know about him. It affirmed that he is an intelligent, friendly, and engaging child, with a fascination for dinosaurs, animals, and numbers. His curiosity is boundless, and his enthusiasm for solving maths problems has to be seen to be believed. Clearly, there is no cause for concern about his capacity for learning.

However, his behaviour was often considered problematic, and he was getting into trouble. A lot. I know I shouldn't have been surprised, but I was. And disappointed. But, logically, he was always going to push against the boundaries of school. He had loved kindy, but I suspect that was mostly because he got to choose what he did and how he did it for the majority of the day. After a rocky start, where he acclimated to the kindy environment by establishing the boundaries in which he could operate, he ruled that playground like a benevolent despot. Everyone got a turn, and everyone could play, so long as he was in charge. He decided the rules, because to accept other people's rules was, of course, abhorrent to him.

WHY BEING GOOD CAN BE BAD FOR YOU

When he started school, Hugo had to test out his new environment. He did this by doing what he does best: mostly suiting himself and seeing what happened. On occasion, he has been in trouble for being rough, but this has, without exception, occurred in the context of sticking up for himself or others. He has never, to my knowledge, physically hurt another child in an unprovoked attack. He also seems to get caught because he is unfailingly honest and admits when he has done the wrong thing.

Contrary to my initial neurotic over-reaction, he did not suddenly become a thug who goes around hurting other children without provocation. My sweet, gentle, loving child, who insists on picking flowers for his teacher every day on his way to school, did not morph into a sociopathic bully with no regard for his classmates or his learning. He has just done school like he does life. Figuring out what he can get away with, and then settling into a form of equilibrium.

In this way, Hugo has taught me a different way of doing life. Whilst I tend to accept rules without question, Hugo tests them out to see how they fit. He accepts consequences without animosity or a grudge and continues to experiment until he figures out how he wants to operate in a given context. He is unapologetic about his desire for an explanation of the rules and reserves the right to disregard rules that don't align with his expectations.

Acknowledging that Hugo is teaching me a different perspective doesn't mean that I want him to be disobedient or disruptive. Nor am I endorsing the vigilante justice model he has sometimes adopted. However, I appreciate his assertiveness in clarifying and testing rules to make sure they are serving their purpose, and his willingness to do the "wrong" thing for the right reason when the need arises. Rather than passively and demurely accepting the rules, Hugo tests them out. At this stage, I feel confident that I don't need to spend any energy worrying about Hugo being too compliant. Ever.

MY GREATEST TEACHER

I am not trying to emulate Hugo but, having experienced many costs as a result of being overly attached to being good, I concede there is definite merit in exploring other options. I admire his ability to explore and create options for himself, even if those options are not strictly within the rules, and I wish I had developed this ability when I was younger. Like any cognitive skill, evaluating a situation and identifying all of the options takes practice. A blind allegiance to the rules negates the need to look for alternatives and leaves us with limited options if the rules stop serving their intended purpose.

When I was in year four, my habitual rule following tendencies resulted in the greatest humiliation my nine-year-old brain could have imagined. To my utter horror and unbearable mortification (then, and for many, many years to come), I wet my pants at school.

It was nearly the end of the day, and my teacher was writing the homework on the blackboard. I had raised my hand to ask to go to the bathroom, but he didn't notice me. The longer my hand went unnoticed, the more desperate and panicked I became.

In that moment, I had no capacity to problem solve or explore possibilities. I was so accustomed to following the rules, that was all I could think of to do. Unfortunately, the standard procedure of getting permission to leave the classroom didn't take into consideration two unexpected factors: an urgent and desperate need to go to the bathroom and an unusually detailed amount of homework to be written on the board.

The hot rush of shame when I lost my battle with my bladder was intense and overwhelming. The bell rang, and my classmates filed out for the day, but I remained seated, frozen and in shock that I had humiliated myself so badly. When my teacher realised what had happened, he was compassionate, concerned, and, understandably, confused. He asked me why I hadn't called out or simply left the room when I realised the urgency of my situation.

Both of those options were perfectly reasonable. However, I can honestly say that neither of them had occurred to me. In that situation of rising panic, my options were biologically restricted to fight, flight, or freeze. Unfortunately for me, the most adaptive of those options (i.e., flight) didn't register as an option. I was so imbued with the need to be good, anything that involved breaking the rules, such as fleeing the classroom without explanation, didn't even register in my consciousness.

It seems absurd, but I genuinely thought the only way I could go to the bathroom was with permission of the teacher. So I followed the rules, raised my hand, and fervently hoped he would notice me. Looking back, I can see how logical it was to simply call out or walk out. There may have been a "please explain" conversation to be had, but no doubt it would have been easily resolved. No big deal, and certainly no lasting impact. However, my good girl brain couldn't process the possibilities, because I was so accustomed to staying within the rules.

Having relived that situation many times over the years, I have discerned that my inaction was not because I was afraid of a consequence. Rather, I genuinely didn't recognise that I had options. I was faced with a situation in which the most reasonable and logical solution happened to be slightly beyond my frame of reference. I was like the Emperor with no clothes. The solution was there. I was just oblivious to it because my good girl worldview was incredibly myopic.

The intensity of the humiliation I experienced in that situation stayed with me for many years, and it is clear that being good did not work in my favour on that day. In this section, I will share the three fundamental attributes that create a foundation from which you can experiment with ways of being, that aren't dictated by the rigid expectations of being good. Breaking up with being good is an ongoing process that requires clarity, confidence, and courage. As you may have guessed, Hugo appears to have these in spades. The next three chapters will examine what each of these involve in the context of breaking up with being good and stepping out of stuckness.

Chapter 6

Clarity – Maximising Discernment

*"Your vision will become clear only when you can look into your own heart.
Who looks outside, dreams; who looks inside, awakes."*

Carl Jung

Clarity: *noun* = the quality or state of being clear; clearness or lucidity as to perception or understanding; freedom from indistinctness or ambiguity.

In the early years of my career, I genuinely loved my job, my students, and my colleagues. Although I was extremely busy, I felt well supported by my organisation. It was challenging, but it felt manageable. I credit much of this to the fact that I trusted my direct supervisor implicitly and was surrounded by a great team of colleagues. Even when things were difficult, we supported each other, and I naively believed that there wouldn't be anything we couldn't handle.

Before I went on maternity leave with Hugo, there were rumblings of organisational change on the horizon, but I was unperturbed. Although the organisation began making somewhat concerning decisions, and I intellectually recognised there would likely be some impact on me at some point, I felt generally buffered from the sharpest edges of the changes. My immediate work environment felt protective, and frankly, I had other things on my mind.

When I returned to work after my maternity leave, I regretted it immediately. My workplace had changed significantly during my 12-month absence, and I felt uneasy and off-centre in what had once been a predictable and comfortable environment. Juggling the demands of a fulltime job and three children was difficult, and to add a bit more spice to the situation, I had returned to a promotion.

My new position carried extra demands and more accountability to a wider array of stakeholders. Some of the flexibility I had previously enjoyed was no longer available, as I was required to attend more meetings in a week than I used to attend in a month. I was sleep-deprived, stressed, and running on close to empty.

I recognise now that I had unrealistic expectations of myself, but it is easy to be wise after the event. My "good employee" schema wouldn't allow being a mother to interfere with my organisational responsibility. My "good mother" schema wouldn't tolerate my children missing out because I had a career. Being so stretched across all domains meant Naggy Nancy was in full voice. Feeling like a hamster on a wheel, I was in perpetual motion. And none of it was good enough for Nancy.

I served on organisational committees and attended their innumerable and, frankly, insufferable, meetings. I wrote lectures and marked assignments on the sidelines of sporting events. I baked cupcakes to be taken to school for birthday celebrations at 11pm. I coached my daughter's netball team. I was on the committee of the netball club. I kept saying yes, even when I desperately wanted to say no. A period of dramatic organisational change compounded my stress and further depleted my resources.

Unsurprisingly, my health and well-being suffered. I experienced a general feeling of malaise, constant headaches, eye inflammations, low energy, susceptibility to repetitive and vicious bacterial infections (one of which led to hospitalisation because it was closing over my throat) and other symptoms that made no sense. I was like a magnet for every virus making its rounds. I was emotionally numb and constantly distracted. I had trouble concentrating, and making decisions felt almost impossible. My emotions felt raw, and my threshold of tolerance was minimal.

Even though I was suffering, I didn't want to stop. I thought I could do it. I thought I could be the good girl and keep on achieving, even in the midst of chaos. I should have listened – to others, to my intuition, to anyone. But I didn't. I wasn't trying to be a martyr. I was genuinely concerned that there was nothing else I could do. And, of course, good girls don't just quit. Also, the sunk cost fallacy had me convinced I would not find anything better.

When I considered the amount of time, energy, focus, and cognitive and emotional resources (not to mention my eye-watering HECS debt) I had invested in my education and my career in academia, it felt impossible to leave. Plus, I was well established in a respected profession. I had colleagues who had become dear friends, and there were many things about my job that I valued. I had flexibility when I needed it. I was in a privileged position where I got to share my knowledge and experience with students. I had credibility, responsibility, and respect.

However, I was using the wrong metrics. I lacked clarity about the true toll of my situation and what really mattered. I overlooked the fact that I was eminently replaceable by any organisation but utterly irreplaceable to my family. I was persisting in a situation that was costing me my well-being and convincing myself that I was doing it for my family.

In my haze of busyness and continuous motion, I failed to see the most important thing. Despite the purity of my intentions, they were not translating into the outcomes I was striving for. There was a disconnect between my intentions and my impact: those whom I was trying to protect and provide for were suffering on my watch.

My breaking point came suddenly and unexpectedly. The faulty reasoning I was using that was driven by the sunk cost fallacy was making everything about me. It clouded my vision and skewed my priorities. What shook me out of that mindset and gave me stunning clarity was the horrifying revelation that Baxter, who was eight at the time, had been mercilessly bullied for a year, and I hadn't known about it.

Whilst I had been feeling tossed about and at the mercy of external forces, so had he. Like me, he had endured, rather than spoken out. He had been threatened into silence and submission and had lived in daily fear for a year. I had known something was wrong, but the truth that was staring me in the face was hidden in plain sight, obscured by busyness and stress and distraction.

During that time, Baxter had changed from a happy, easygoing child who enjoyed school and loved learning, to a sullen and irritable complainer. He reported frequent headaches, was unreasonable, volatile, and didn't want to go to school. He objected vehemently to having to attend after school care, and when I picked him up, he would often refuse to tell me anything about his day. This coincided with a major project at work, which required me to work longer hours. Longer hours for me meant more time at after school care for Baxter, and this was when his bully terrorised him the most.

When we got home each day, he would routinely rush to the toilet with desperate urgency. I would often ask him why he didn't just go at after school care. His non-committal response offered little explanation. *"Dunno. Just don't want to,"* was always accompanied by a dismissive shoulder shrug. He started asking for the light to be kept on at night, despite having outgrown night lights a few years prior. Sometimes, he would ask if he could sleep in Maddi's room, much to her ten-year-old outrage. She didn't want to share a room with her brother. He didn't give a compelling reason why, so the matter was dropped.

I had searched for an explanation for his symptoms. At one point I thought perhaps it was a developmental thing, as I knew seven-year-olds can sometimes be difficult. I remembered reading somewhere that the odd ages of childhood often coincided with changes in temperament. That had been somewhat true when Maddi was seven, so that possibility remained feasible. Even though Baxter wasn't seven anymore, I thought perhaps it was a delayed onset of whatever it is that makes seven-year-olds cantankerous. He also had recurring tonsillitis, so that seemed like another reasonable explanation. Then he broke his arm, which meant he couldn't do many of the things he enjoyed. Another excellent explanation for his dark moods and unpleasant temperament.

Just in case it was something else, I had taken him to see a GP, paediatrician, physiotherapist, optometrist, and acupuncturist.

He had blood tests, x-rays, and numerous examinations. None of these health professionals could find an explanation for his symptoms. Obviously, terror doesn't show up on an x-ray or a blood test, so there were no answers to be found there.

Baxter's tonsils had been removed in the last week of the previous year of school. He had spent the Christmas holidays recuperating and, it seemed, regaining his sweet temperament. He was no longer volatile or irritable, and our kind and thoughtful boy was back. It makes total sense that a two-month break from his aggressor would be of tremendous benefit to him, but of course we still didn't know anything about the bullying. Unfortunately, it didn't take long for the healing that had happened over the holidays to become undone.

In the second week back at school, Maddi and Baxter got into a vicious fight. Over toothpaste. This, in and of itself, may not seem untoward. However, the viciousness of this fight was highly unusual. Baxter, who is a pacifist by nature and insists that we relocate, rather than kill, spiders and bugs in our house, had his fist up to his sister's face, threatening to punch her. Seeing his face taut with aggression, and Maddi's shock and confusion, rang alarm bells. That confrontation was so out of character; it demanded answers. This wasn't about the toothpaste.

I sent Baxter to his room to calm down and asked Maddi for her version of events. The kids had been discussing Maddi's recent appointment as a school captain. Historically, Baxter had always been proud of his sister's accomplishments. On this occasion, however, he was scathing and critical and told her that she was going to be a crap school captain. He accused her of being "up herself" and said that nobody was going to take any notice of her. Stung and shocked by this uncharacteristic tirade, Maddi had snatched the toothpaste and refused to give it to him until he apologised. Baxter refused, Maddi insisted, and the fist-to-the-face scenario ensued.

In the hour that followed, I got Baxter's version of the story. And it broke my heart. Initially, he maintained that he did think Maddi was going to be a crap school captain, and he hadn't said sorry because he wasn't. I was met with repeated denials that there was anything wrong. His arms were crossed, his face was tense, and he glowered at me from behind a mask I didn't recognise. However, there was such a misalignment between his words, his physiology, and who I knew him to be, that I persisted in my questioning.

After an extended period of time, where he steadfastly maintained that there was nothing I needed to know and he just wanted to punch Maddi in the face because she took the toothpaste, I was almost ready to give up. Although I couldn't reconcile those words with the gentle, loving child who always asked the barber for an extra lollipop for his sister, he was holding the line, and I couldn't penetrate his defences. Ready to concede, I observed that the words coming out of his mouth didn't sound like his.

"Buddy, I'm so confused. The words coming out of your mouth don't sound like they belong to you. It's your voice, but they don't sound like your words."

This observation clearly rang true for him. It initiated the release of an absolute torrent of emotion, the depth and intensity of which I have never seen from Baxter, before or since. His anguish was immense, as he acknowledged those words were not his. They were his bully's, and they were just one instalment in a year-long episode of relentless bullying he had endured in silence.

The reason Baxter had regained his gentle disposition over the holidays was more than the sun, sand, and fun of the Christmas break. It was the reprieve from living in fear, each and every day. After just two weeks back at school, the bullying was happening again, and Baxter had lost capacity to keep it inside.

From the avalanche of emotion spewing forth, everything became crystal clear. The mood swings, the irritability, and the volatility were all products of living in constant hypervigilance. The running to the toilet each day was a consequence of his unwillingness to use the bathrooms at school, for fear of being found alone and vulnerable by his bully. His desire to sleep in Maddi's room was based on a threat from his bully that he knew where we lived, and he was coming to hurt our family. Nothing was off limits to this bully. Threats were made against all of us, and Baxter felt unsafe at school and at home.

Baxter's bully had described in excruciating detail the location and extent of the beating he was going to give Baxter. He just didn't tell him when; leaving Baxter in a constant state of fear. He also tormented Baxter with explicit threats against Maddi, and against me, the nature of which were too horrific for Baxter to put into words. I deduced from the context that they were threats beyond the realm of what a child of that age should have knowledge, let alone an intention to perpetrate. With each agonising detail, my heart broke a little more. And my clarity sharpened.

I knew immediately that something had to change. Obviously, the bullying needed to be addressed at school, but that was not enough. I needed to make a fundamental change to my life so I could be the parent my children needed me to be. I had been so busy trying to be ok when I was overwhelmed and burning out, that I hadn't been able to put the pieces together to draw what was an obvious conclusion. I knew he was suffering. I just didn't see why, until I did. He was terrified. All the time.

I was faced with an agonising juxtaposition. My good girl schemas for an academic and its counterpart for a parent were clashing terribly. My tendencies toward perfectionism and people pleasing had created a perfect storm where I felt constantly caught between the demands of those roles. By saying yes to the wrong things (everything that was asked of me), and no to the wrong things (self-care and compassion), I had taken myself way out of alignment.

I could not be the parent or the employee that I wanted to be when I was so physically, emotionally, and psychologically depleted. I could not allow my children to bear the burden of my misplaced adherence to unsustainable schemas. Deciding to change for my kids was a no-brainer but identifying what that meant was initially a mystery. However, I recognised two important processes that would enhance my clarity: tuning into intuition and examining the expectations.

Tune into intuition

Tuning into intuition might sound like a bunch of "woo woo", but it doesn't have to be. Rather than some esoteric practice reserved for the most spiritual among us, it can be as simple as taking notice of the clues your body sends you that help you know things without knowing how. That feeling of discomfort in your body when something seems off. That hesitation to walk down that path when there is nothing obviously ominous. That "no" feeling you get when you meet someone, but quickly brush aside because you don't want to be judgmental. The scratchy, irritable feeling when someone wants you to do something and you can't think of a good reason for your reluctance.

Specialists in self-protection who work with victims of crime report that, almost without exception, those who experienced a serious attack had some inkling before the event that something wasn't right. Whether it was a hesitation to step into a lift with the man who would become their attacker, or a sense that there was something off about the customer who would ultimately hold them at gunpoint, their bodies responded in a way that made sense only after the fact. The advice from these survivors is consistent: trust your instincts.

This is an example of tuning into intuition when the stakes are high and the consequences of not doing so are severe. However, we are given clues by our bodies all the time. We just tend not to listen to them. Often, our reluctance to listen to our intuition is rooted in our desire to be good. We don't want to cause upset or offence by refusing to get into the lift with someone who makes us feel uncomfortable. We shrug it off, and perhaps admonish ourselves for being judgmental. We may also insist on more tactile evidence than intuition can offer. We are so accustomed to thinking, that we can lose some of the wisdom of feeling.

I have spent a lot of time in my head. That is a logical outcome from spending many, many years in and around universities. In an environment where you need to justify everything with evidence, this works well. When operating from your intellect, your decisions are made after careful examination of the evidence, and if required, you can provide a clear articulation of your rationale for the choices you make. In many instances, whatever you say in academia has to have been said by someone else in order to be credible. If you can't cite it, you can't say it.

Following that logic, it made complete sense for me to follow the established career path for academics. Being good meant ticking every box and exceeding every expectation, to ensure I navigated the clearly delineated pathway to success. It also explains why I felt so compelled to do all the things good mothers do. The problem was, I had signed myself up for the perfectionist's version of two fulltime workloads.

I looked at the objectively agreed-upon criteria for success in academia, and the, albeit subjective, but easily recognised, criteria of success in motherhood, and assumed I had to do it all. And more. My intuition told me it was too much, but I had learned to turn down the volume on that. I was all about the evidence: tangible, measurable outcomes, rather than feelings or the sense that something was off.

CLARITY – MAXIMISING DISCERNMENT

Since leaving academia, I have done a lot of unlearning. Reflecting on the many missed opportunities to identify what had been going on with Baxter, I have recognised that I have overemphasised my intellect and squashed my intuition, to my own detriment, and that of my family. There have been many times when I have had a nagging feeling that I was making a poor decision or missing something. Instead of listening to that small feeling, I would rationalise my way out of the situation.

I have realised that one of the reasons it is so comfortable to rely on your intellect at the expense of your intuition is because there is fear and risk in going with your intuition. There is no empirical evidence to use in support of your decision. It is all you, only you. So, if it turns out to be a poor decision, it's on you. For a good girl, that's a lot of pressure!

I have had to acknowledge that I crave the security of evidence. That way, even if it turns out to be a poor decision, there's no shame in it. Anyone with that information would have made that choice too. It doesn't reflect badly on me personally. So, apparently, I would prefer to make a sensible poor choice than an intuitive good choice. That's something I'm working on.

When I allow myself to tune into my intuition, and be informed by my intellect, I am much more likely to have clarity about what the next best step is. As frightening as it might be, I can't help but agree with Glennon Doyle, who said: *"It's nearly impossible to blaze one's own path while following in someone else's footsteps."*[6] Giving yourself permission to trust your own intuition can feel foreign, but ultimately, it is much more likely to take you where you need to go.

---

[6] Doyle, G. (2020) *Untamed.* New York: The Dial Press.

Examine the expectations

Have you ever noticed how expectations are like lurkers, hanging around in the background, mostly on the periphery of your awareness? They tend to only get noticed when they aren't met. The problem with expectations is that we all have them, and we are mostly oblivious to them. It is not until our expectations are challenged that we realise they exist. This means that we are often making decisions without really thinking about why we do what we do.

On the one hand, this is essential. Our brains are bombarded with millions of discrete pieces of information at any given moment, and the only way we can make sense of the world is to filter the vast majority of that information out of our awareness. We cannot consciously decide where to direct all of our attention, so our brains do it for us. We give clues about what we value, and our brain brings us more of that.

We also have access to a number of mechanisms which support these broader cognitive capacities to navigate our sensorially overloaded environment. For example, heuristics, which are basically mental shortcuts, help us to make decisions quickly. Based on previous experiences and knowledge, heuristics enable us to quickly make sense of a situation and decide in an efficient and (somewhat) effective manner.

However, there is a catch. Whilst heuristics can make us efficient decision makers, they can also lead to cognitive biases. This means that we make decisions based on things which appear obvious or meaningful to us in that moment, rather than evaluating all of the possibilities we could consider. In essence, the decisions we make in the present are close replicas of decisions we have made previously, even if the circumstances are different.

CLARITY – MAXIMISING DISCERNMENT

In the same way, when we have strong or rigid beliefs about the way things "are" or "should be" (puritanical perspective), we can easily find confirmation for our perspective. When we ascribe to the need to be good, we can easily find reinforcement for this belief. We surround ourselves with people who think like us. We are drawn to examples of others who are emulating those ideals. We also compare ourselves to those exemplars and find ourselves lacking. When examining the expectations we are inadvertently holding ourselves up to, it is helpful to consider not only *what* we believe, but also *why* we believe it.

Like tuning into intuition, examining our expectations is an opportunity to attain clarity about what is driving our choices. If we are overly attached to fulfilling the demands of an unrealistic and possibly outdated schema of being good, these processes provide the means to consider alternatives.

For me, getting clarity about the misalignment between my intention and my impact was life-altering. Although the clues were all there, I just wasn't attuned to them. It took a defining life event to shake my vision clear, and to illuminate the importance of remaining mindful about what success metrics I am using. As with the most painful lessons, it is one I have learned well.

Chapter 7

Confidence – Enhancing Certainty

"Confidence comes not from always being right but from not fearing to be wrong."

Peter T. McIntyre

Confidence: *noun* = a feeling or consciousness of one's powers or of reliance on one's circumstances; the quality or state of being certain.

In an episode of Oprah's Masterclass, author Elizabeth Gilbert told a story about how one of her audience members made her cry. In the aftermath of her success with international bestseller, "Eat, Pray, Love," Gilbert had been on tour, presenting a talk about finding your passion. In her talk, she shared how her passion for writing had been a driving force in her life for as long as she could remember. She had been so committed to her craft that she was willing to work all day and write all night, even if nobody was ever going to read what she had written. Her story was inspirational and compelling, with a clear message: find what you love, work hard, don't allow obstacles to interfere, and you will succeed.

After giving this talk to an audience in Australia, Gilbert received an email. In that email, an audience member shared her despair. She told Gilbert that she had been desperately trying to find her passion, and she had not succeeded. Her hope in attending Gilbert's talk had been to find encouragement, but she left feeling worse than she had when she arrived.

The reason for her despondence was that Gilbert's story of triumph through persistence reinforced the audience member's feelings of inadequacy. Although it was not Gilbert's intention, the message this audience member had received was that there is one all-consuming thing for everyone, and that is your only path to success. Until you find your special thing, you have nothing. Unfortunately, this audience member didn't have her special thing, so she felt like she had nothing.

This perspective was eye-opening for Gilbert. For someone who had been gifted with clarity and certainty about her passion, the idea of not having a passion was new and different. Her talk had been developed authentically from her personal experience and had genuinely inspired many. However, it did not capture the experience of those who did not have a single, driving passion. Inspired by that perspective-shifting, and tear-inducing email, Gilbert developed a new talk. When she reflected on the people she admired and loved the most, she realised that they represented the possibility that there were multiple pathways to success.

In her new talk, Gilbert used the analogy of jackhammers and hummingbirds. Jackhammers are focused. They choose a path and they are relentless in their commitment to breaking through in that space. They are the single-passion creatures like Gilbert: blessed with a singular purpose and focus. For them, success is mostly linear – they succeed through persistence. The purpose of their journey is to get them to their destination. In contrast, hummingbirds flit from one thing to the next. They are curious creatures who never stay in one place for long. They explore and experiment, and they thrive on variety. For hummingbirds, the journey *is* the destination.

I find this metaphor reassuring, as it reminds us that it is not essential to have one driving passion, the absence of which equates to having no purpose. When cultivating confidence to make a change, we don't have to wait for our one life-defining, great idea before we get started. Recognising that some of us may be hummingbirds is liberating, as it relinquishes the urgency to figure out what we want to do and be when we grow up before we start the process of pursuing our dreams.

Although I have demonstrated jackhammer qualities at times, by focusing on a goal and pursuing it, I also embody some hummingbird characteristics. In fact, I think the hummingbird approach is my default. However, like the audience member who wrote to Liz Gilbert, I have, at times, felt frustrated at my lack of clarity about what I wanted to be when I grew up. The lack of clarity has resulted in low confidence, and a feeling of deficit. I had bought into the myth that having a singular passion and focus meant being good and was the way to become successful. Each time those pesky hummingbird characteristics re-emerged, I felt uncomfortable because they took me away from that ideal.

For many years, I was embarrassed that I had experimented with a number of university courses before I completed an undergraduate degree. Absurdly, I thought that not knowing what I wanted to do for the rest of my life when I finished school at 17 indicated that I was flaky or indecisive. My good girl schema had me convinced that I should find one thing and pursue it. Each time I tried something new, there was a part of me that thought I was crazy. Why couldn't I just make a decision and stick with it? Perhaps it's because I am more hummingbird than jackhammer, and also because there is no rule that says you have to pick a lane and stay in it forever.

I also experienced some dissonance about this in my academic role. So many aspects of psychology fascinated me; I didn't want to just pick one topic. I enjoyed teaching many subjects and conducted research in a variety of areas. Part of this was pragmatic, as I collaborated with others, and was happy to explore topics that made sense to the team, but it was also because I was interested in many things. However, in academia, this is not a recommended strategic approach. Variety in your research topics looks like indecision and detracts from your capacity to be considered an expert. The most applauded (and funded) research profiles are linear and niched, producing a track record that is logical and streamlined.

Interestingly, the phrase, *"jack of all trades, master of none"* has been used as a way of disparaging and discouraging what I now think of as hummingbird behaviour. However, there is more to that saying. Although there is a lack of consensus about which version is the original, there is an alternative version of that saying: *"A jack of all trades is a master of none, but often times better than a master of one."* Regardless of its origin, recognising that there are benefits to having many skills and interests, and that a lack of singular purpose is not a deficit, is encouraging. I hope it is also confidence enhancing for the hummingbirds in our midst.

It is easy to consider the path of the jackhammer to be most aligned to being good, especially as it epitomises the traditional model of a successful career. For many of us, "climbing the career ladder" represents an essential component of our grown-up goals. How high the ladder goes may differ, but there has been some consensus that a singular, linear, upwards trajectory of incremental improvement is expected. That is the path of the good employee.

In previous eras, where individuals worked in the same company or industry for decades and success meant working your way through the ranks and retiring with a gold watch, this metaphor was perfect. However, I would like to suggest that this metaphor is no longer an adequate representation of the typical career journey. Further, clinging to this metaphor is reinforcing the fear and uncertainty that accompanies career changes which, in the rapidly changing world of work, are inevitable. Plus, it makes hummingbirds feel like losers.

The problem with this metaphor is twofold. Firstly, it suggests that there is a single "right" path, and once you are on it, you shouldn't get off. Such a narrow view is, in my opinion, limiting and disempowering and disenfranchises jackhammers and hummingbirds alike. Whilst the passion and focus of the jackhammers can be a pathway to success, it is not the only one. Rather than expecting each individual to have a singular focus, passion, and purpose, I believe it is entirely possible for each of us to have many offerings to the world.

The second major problem with the ladder metaphor is that the only type of career change it can comfortably accommodate is that which moves us vertically. We move up via a promotion or an increase in clients, revenue, or some other meaningful metric to measure an improvement in our position. We move down when things don't go to plan, and this is typically viewed as some sort of failure. Either way, the path doesn't differ; merely our position relative to our start and end point on the ladder.

The reality of modern life is that change is constant, multidimensional, and often out of our control. For the modern professional, change is the norm, not the exception, and most of us in the workforce today will experience many significant career changes. This means that the complex pathways that comprise a career are not well captured with the metaphor of the career ladder. It also means that who want to be good and not step outside the norm stay stuck in positions they no longer want.

Instead of conceptualising a successful career trajectory as climbing a ladder, I prefer to think of it as navigating a jungle gym. The complex structure of the jungle gym, which has no clear path to the top, nor even an imperative to get to the top, is a much more apt descriptor of the modern career; and it has room and scope for jackhammers and hummingbirds alike. It opens up the possibility that going in a different direction is not a bad thing. You can legitimately explore horizontally or diagonally – you don't just have to focus on the vertical trajectory. You can hang upside down to gain a different perspective, or merely enjoy the view from where you find yourself in the current moment. A single, linear path to the top is no longer a prerequisite for success.

Many of my clients are facing an intersection in their career. These changes are often accompanied by tremendous angst. There is fear associated with uncertainty and the potential for many losses: identity, traction, credibility, authority. For some, like me, it can represent an existential crisis.

These fears are legitimate and debilitating. They are also associated with the preconceived notion that a career ladder is the correct path and that being good only means moving up. When you focus on a singular pathway, akin to the career ladder, any obstacle you encounter leaves you with few options: try to go up in spite of the obstacle (often at considerable cost), go back (which is equated with failure), or stay stuck.

Not so with the jungle gym. Upon encountering an obstacle, you can explore the opportunities to move in many different directions, as the broader perspective offered by the jungle gym inevitably includes many alternative paths. You don't have to get off the jungle gym when you encounter an obstacle: you simply pivot and find another way.

So, whether you are a jackhammer or a hummingbird, I encourage you to consider the opportunities of the jungle gym, rather than the ladder. The journey becomes much more enjoyable when there are multiple options available to you. Making a change, whether self-initiated or as a matter of necessity, doesn't have to feel like you are on the bottom rung of the ladder again. Rather, the view from a different position on the jungle gym may be just the perspective shift you didn't know you were looking for.

I believe it is helpful to recognise the differences between hummingbirds and jackhammers in this chapter about confidence because we lack confidence when we lack certainty. This can be a genuine disadvantage to the hummingbirds. If they are trying to be a jackhammer and find their singular purpose, they may feel frustrated and deficient. However, if they appreciate that their challenge in choosing is actually their gift, they can feel much more confident about their curiosity about many things.

Jackhammers also need confidence. However, they derive it from having clarity about their purpose and taking steps to get closer to achieving that goal. Knowing what they want to do gives them the certainty that they can pursue that purpose. They may encounter setbacks in the pursuit of their purpose, but they have the strength of their convictions to keep them on track. I suspect Thomas Edison's willingness to generate 10,000 prototypes was influenced by an unwavering conviction that he could find the solution.

If you have been in a situation where you have felt like you were lacking confidence, you may have been advised to: *"fake it until you make it"*. Although I understand the sentiment behind this phrase, I find it a bit gross. For the good girl who likes to do things properly, faking it feels inauthentic and uncomfortable. I prefer the alternative: *"practise it until you believe it"*.

Although it may only be semantics, I find this alternative much more empowering. If you frame the new skill/role/situation as something you are "practising", you give yourself permission to suck a bit at first, but also instil an expectation and belief that you will improve. When you are learning or trying something new, it's ok to find it difficult. However, the more you practise, the better you will become, and the more you will believe you can do it. In this way, you can enhance your confidence by doing.

The Conscious Competence model[7] is a helpful framework for understanding how we learn and also creating confidence. The four stages of this model are:

1. **Unconscious incompetence** – we don't know what we don't know.

2. **Conscious incompetence** – we start to learn and become aware of what we don't know.

3. **Conscious competence** – we acquire the ability to perform a task but have to concentrate/focus – it is not automatic.

4. **Unconscious competence** – we become skilled at the task and can do it unconsciously/automatically.

---

[7] This model is well known and commonly used in psychology. Noel Burch, an employee of Gordon Training International in the 1970s is generally credited with the original description of this model.

This model can be helpful in enhancing confidence because it normalises the process of mastery and certainty. If we consider these four stages on a continuum, it is reasonable to expect that, at any given time, we can be on a different phase of the continuum for a range of skills. This needn't be a cause for concern.

We can feel confident that, even if we are in the uncomfortable stage of conscious incompetence (the least preferred stage), we are on the path to mastery. Whether it is learning a new skill or figuring out who we want to be when we grow up (or in our second, third or fourth career), confidence comes from trying, experimenting, and integrating the feedback we acquire.

This means that, rather than waiting to feel confident before we try new things, we can try new things and trust that we will gain confidence as we acquire competence. For jackhammers and hummingbirds alike, there is freedom in recognising that we don't have to decide on what we are going to be good at before we attempt it. The confidence comes from the doing, which is made possible by attaining clarity about what really matters. Together, clarity and confidence enhance the third fundamental attribute for exploring possibilities beyond the status quo: courage.

Chapter 8

Courage – Harnessing Conviction

"Life shrinks or expands in proportion to one's courage."

Anaïs Nin

Courage: *noun* = the ability to do something that frightens one; bravery.

When I was paralysed with indecision about my future, and feeling afraid and uncertain, I thought a lot about courage: what it is; what it isn't; how to get it. In the course of those musings, I realised that the presence of fear doesn't necessarily mean you need to cultivate courage. Fear can be present because what you are thinking of doing is a bad idea. That fear is intuitive and adaptive. It helps us avoid choices which are not in our best interests. The best response to that kind of fear is acknowledgement and gratitude.

However, fear can also be present because what you are thinking of doing is a new idea. Our brains are programmed to keep us safe, so things which are new and unfamiliar can be deemed a threat. However, sometimes those new ideas are the best ones, and it is those kinds of ideas which require courage.

It is also worth remembering that the presence of courage doesn't mean the process of change won't be challenging. Transitions are tough, and unbecoming something so you can become something else is uncomfortable. One of the best metaphors for this is the lifecycle of the butterfly.

Life lessons from entomology

When Baxter was three, he asked me how a caterpillar becomes a butterfly. I must admit that entomology is not my thing, but I was confident I had this covered. Although I had never really given the lifecycle of a butterfly too much thought, what I had done was read, *"The Very Hungry Caterpillar"* approximately 5000 times. All of my kids have loved that book, and, in my mind, that investment of time was paying dividends. I was surprised that Baxter had forgotten the story but happy to share my superior entomological knowledge with him.

"Remember, the caterpillar gets really hungry and eats a lot, builds itself a cocoon, goes inside for two weeks, and then it comes out as a beautiful butterfly."

I was pleased with my concise yet accurate summary of the book. I hadn't quoted verbatim (although I could have!), but it was extremely on point. That self-satisfaction was misplaced and short-lived. I should have known. Baxter doesn't forget anything. He didn't need a reminder of what the book said. He wanted to actually *know* what happened. As in, the biological process, not the storybook narration.

"But what does the caterpillar do inside the cocoon? How does it grow its wings? Were the wings already there? Does it hurt when they grow? Is it like getting a new tooth?"

As is often the case when Baxter asks me questions, I had no idea. As is also the case when Baxter asks me questions and I have to find an answer which satisfies him (which typically means something with a citation as proof that I didn't make it up), I learn interesting things. On this occasion, I learned that the caterpillar doesn't grow wings to become a butterfly.

The caterpillar dies to become a butterfly. More specifically, the caterpillar digests itself via enzymes. Through that process, hormones are released, and it is from those hormones that the butterfly develops. This process is why butterflies are such a powerful symbol of new beginnings. A butterfly is not a caterpillar with wings. It is an entirely new creature, created by the obliteration of its previous form.

I can't think of a better metaphor to capture the process of change. Undoing is uncomfortable. It can feel like you are losing defining characteristics; parts of you that make you who you are. For me, changing my career required an undoing of a significant chunk of my identity. I didn't know how to complete the identity card on an international flight, because I was stumped when it asked me to list my profession. I had spent such a long time defining myself as an academic, I didn't know who I was when I wasn't that. Moving away from the familiar, even when it's toxic, is scary and makes you miss things that you didn't even really value when you had them. Absence makes the heart grow fonder; undoing makes you crave familiarity.

Another important lesson from butterflies is that they need to engage in a struggle to emerge from their cocoon to develop the strength they require to fly. Without that struggle to strengthen their wings, they will die. This gives a whole new appreciation for the idea that there are gifts that only become available as a result of a struggle. Butterflies are born from destruction and must engage in a struggle in order to survive, which makes them a perfect metaphor for personal growth and change. Together, these lessons from entomology give important clues about courage.

Burn the boats

Prior to finalising my decision to leave my career in academia, I took some time off. Whilst I was on leave, I did a lot of thinking and reflecting on my future. I had recognised that I needed to make a change, but the reality was that life after academia was completely uncertain and, frankly, terrifying. Logically, I recognised that there must be something else for me. I just couldn't discern what it was. My brain was overloaded with reasons why I should stick with the safety of the familiar, even though it wasn't working for me anymore.

When I created a list of the pros and cons of staying, I realised that all of the reasons to stay were based on fear. *What if I can't find anything else? What if I do find something else and I'm unhappy? What if my commute is too long? What if I have no flexibility? What if I don't make any friends?* And so on. Underlying all of these fears was the core fear with which we all grapple at some point: *What if I'm not enough?* The rest were just excuses to keep me stuck. Consistent with its mandate of keeping me safe, my brain was throwing up all sorts of reasons to fear the unknown and thus stay in the safety of the familiar.

However, the reasons not to stay carried the promise of something better. They also aligned with my most important list of non-negotiables and must-haves: my health and my family. I allowed myself to ponder. *What if I could design a career that worked for me and my family? What if I could keep all the best bits of my career and ditch the rest?* These were intriguing possibilities and definitely shifted my focus towards finding the courage to leave, rather than settling for staying stuck.

As is often the case when we are preparing to be courageous, and are firmly in the grips of fear, the strength of our conviction will be tested. At around the time I had decided that the best thing for my health and my family was for me to leave academia, I received a phone call that caused me to carefully consider whether or not I was sure about my decision.

A high-ranking official from my organisation telephoned me unexpectedly. She wanted to check in with me to see how I was going. I was extremely touched at her thoughtfulness. She also expressed her appreciation for my many contributions to the university and told me that I was a valued member of the team. Her spontaneous kindness was a balm I didn't know I was craving. And it nearly brought me undone.

I went from feeling certain that my career in academia was no longer tenable, to contemplating brushing aside all that I knew to be true about the toll my job was taking on my health and my family. Feeling valued and needed and wanted was like an opiate to a recovering addict. I had survived without it for a long time, but I really liked the feeling when I got it back again. My fear about my future was intense, and I allowed myself to indulge in the fantasy that things weren't really all that bad. I started thinking things like:

With such nice people in my organisation, surely I could find a way to continue?

Perhaps I had exaggerated, or over-reacted, or imagined the severity of my burnout?

Baxter's bullying has stopped, and he doesn't appear overly traumatised. Maybe I was being too dramatic?

And that's where I caught myself. When I realised that my fear was intense enough to try to convince me to sacrifice my child's well-being so that I could avoid the unknown, I knew that fear wasn't in alignment with my values. It was the kind of fear that needed to be met with courage. I needed to feel the fear and do it anyway. I needed to burn the boats, and commit to the change, no matter how afraid I felt. Like the caterpillar that submits to the process of metamorphosis to become a butterfly, and the butterfly that commits to the struggle to break free from its chrysalis, I had to go all in. Terrified or not.

So where does courage come from? For me, it comes from clarity about what really matters and the confidence that what I am intending to do is aligned with my values. When you know why you are choosing to do something, and that reason is compelling enough, it takes you beyond your fear. Courage is the willingness to do the hard thing, because you know doing it afraid is more important than avoiding the fear by not doing it.

If I hadn't been absolutely certain that my previously comfortable career was no longer tenable, I would still be there. I have no doubt about that. Walking away from my career was, without question, one of the most frightening decisions I have ever made. I definitely didn't *feel* courageous. I felt afraid.

To go back to our caterpillar to a butterfly metaphor, I was a caterpillar looking for the opt out clause on the "dying to myself to emerge as something new" mandate. Part of me wanted to just forget the bad stuff and stay where I was. However, I knew that, scared or not, I had to submit to my process of metamorphosis. Although easier said than done, clarity leads to confidence, which leads to courage. And that's how you find your wings.

Part 3

Stepping out of Stuckness - Adopting an ASTUTE Mindset

Introduction to the ASTUTE Transformation Framework

"If you can change your mind, you can change your life."

William James

When I founded Astute Consulting Services, I chose the name because "astute" means, among other things, "able to accurately assess situations or people," "discerning," "having good judgement," and "being perceptive". These are all characteristics I seek to bring in service of my clients, so the name seemed apt. Over time, the word astute has also provided the basis for a transformative framework that has been extremely helpful in supporting my clients (and myself) to thrive during times of transition.

Based on a combination of neuroscience and a bit of intuition, the ASTUTE Transformation Framework is not intended to exclusively apply to the process of breaking up with being good. Rather, it is helpful whenever you are seeking to make any substantial positive change. Although each element of the framework can stand alone, for simplicity and completeness, it is best to implement each element in the order in which it is presented.

The ASTUTE Transformation Framework is as follows:

A = ALIGN: Getting in alignment requires clarity about what matters most. Some important elements to getting in alignment include values, vision, purpose, mission and a personalised definition of success.

Key question: *What really matters to me and how do I define success?*

S = SET INTENTIONS: Intentions set the tone for goals. Identifying how you want to "be," before you focus on what you want to "do" is a powerful way of enhancing the likelihood of achieving your definition of success.

Key question: What do I commit to BEING first, and DOING second, in order to achieve my definition of success?

T = THANKFULNESS: The importance of gratitude cannot be overestimated. Research has demonstrated that gratitude is a powerful influencer of well-being[8], and there is an emerging body of research investigating the ways in which gratitude may influence the structure and function of our brains[9].

Key question: What can I be grateful for, in this moment?

U = UNDO: In order to implement meaningful change, it is important to identify what we need to stop doing. This creates room for the new habits that are fundamental to success and allows us to grow and change in ways that align with our desired way of being.

Key question: What is getting in my way and how can I stop sabotaging myself?

---

[8] Wood, A. M., Froh, J. J., and Geraghty, A. W. A. (2010). Gratitude and well-being: A review and theoretical integration. *Clin. Psychol. Rev.* 30, 890-905. doi: 10.1016/j.cpr.2010.03.005

[9] Karns, C.M., Moore, W.E., & Ulrich, M. (2017). The cultivation of pure altruism via gratitude: A Functional MRI study of change with gratitude practice. *Frontiers in Human Neuroscience*, 11. DOI=10.3389/fnhum.2017.00599

T = TOGETHER: Research has demonstrated that one of the best predictors of longevity is social connection[10]. It has also been noted that true excellence rarely occurs in a silo. Identifying the core people with whom we can/should connect is crucial.

Key question: Who are my people? How can I connect with them?

E = ELEVATE: The best bit: making small, incremental changes that collectively improve your quality of life.

Key question: What can I do today that I will thank myself for tomorrow?

The beauty of these six principles is that they apply equally to individuals and groups, in times of normal transition and in times of chaos. In its totality, the ASTUTE Transformation Framework is intended to promote individual and collective thriving, by recognising that we all do better when we have a clear understanding of what matters most to us, an actionable plan for achieving our own definition of success, and an appreciation of the ways in which we are all inextricably linked.

---

[10] Harvard Study of Adult Development: https://www.adultdevelopmentstudy.org/

Chapter 9

Align – Identifying Your Non-Negotiables and Deal-Breakers

"Just as your car runs more smoothly and requires less energy to go faster and farther when the wheels are in perfect alignment, you perform better when your thoughts, feelings, emotions, goals, and values are in balance."

Brian Tracy

Align: *verb* = to put two or more things into a straight line; to change something so that it has a correct relationship to something else.

Getting into alignment means getting clarity about what is true, important, and necessary for you to be authentically yourself. It also requires a clear and personal definition of success. This is in contrast with a contrived version of you that you think is meeting other people's expectations.

Marie Kondo recommends you examine every possession and check if it brings you joy. I recommend you do this for your life. This process involves a deliberate, honest, and thorough examination of all facets of your life. It requires you to look into the mirror (literally or metaphorically) and ask yourself some tough questions, including but not limited to:

What do I stand for?

What are my values?

What are my aspirations?

What are the success metrics I am using? Are they mine or someone else's?

What are my non-negotiables?

What are my deal-breakers?

Am I motivated by fear or possibility?

Am I maintaining a persona or living authentically?

Am I compelled by the tyranny of the goods (or even the shoulds)?

Do I define myself by the roles I perform or the person I am?

Conducting a life inventory of this nature can be both confronting and illuminating. This process is a way of getting clarity about what you *think* you know about what is important, and why/how you think you know it. It requires you to challenge your own assumptions and provides an opportunity to identify the expectations you have been striving to meet (whether you realised it or not).

This type of self-reflection is often done in the context of a major life upheaval, but you don't have to wait for something drastic to take that look into the mirror. It is also not something that you do once and forget about it. Just as the wheels on a car need realigning over time, it is worthwhile checking your personal alignment periodically. Whilst there are many ways you can do this, here are a few ideas that I have found helpful.

Clues for checking your alignment:

1. Name your values

One of the key elements of this process is identifying your values. Whilst we all have values, and they undoubtedly influence our behaviour, making your core values salient is a powerful way of simplifying and improving your decisions. When you identify your core values, they become your decision-making framework. Each time you are faced with a difficult choice, the option which aligns most closely with your core values is the one which is most likely best for you. It was precisely this process which helped me to recognise when I needed to change my career.

Whilst my job met many of my needs, goals, and even aspirations, the fact that it was doing so at the expense of my health and well-being meant that it was no longer aligned. Although I hadn't considered health and well-being to be values (although, they can and probably should be), two of my core values were family and excellence.

In this context, excellence doesn't mean achievement or being *the* best. It means living in a way that is conducive to being *my* best, and that clearly wasn't the case when I was experiencing burnout. Also, the obvious cost to my family of me being unwell and burnt out meant that my career and my values were not properly aligned.

There are many lists of values that have been collated and are readily available. I recommend taking the time to have a look for one, and spending some time clarifying your core values. Alternatively, you can generate your own list simply by asking yourself: "What really matters to me?" repeatedly until you have a list that feels complete. If you use somebody else's list, it is likely that you will agree with most, if not all of the values listed.

The idea is to identify the ones that resonate most strongly for you – you *feel* their importance, rather than merely recognise or understand it intellectually. You can see how those values have influenced your decisions, even if you weren't aware of their impact. Try to narrow your list down to the smallest number possible. You will probably find that your top ten (or so) can be mapped to your top three or four values, creating a hierarchy. This is helpful, because it can provide the point of differentiation if your decisions are particularly complicated.

2. The Six Universal Human Needs

According to Human Needs Psychology, there are six human needs which are universal. As taught by Tony Robbins, this theory identifies the six universal human needs as: certainty, variety, significance, love/connection, growth, and contribution. Whilst the first four are considered necessary for survival, growth and contribution are considered essential for thriving.

According to this theory, every human shares these needs. However, the emphasis we place on the various needs differs, as does the way in which we ensure these needs are met. Each of them can be met in either healthy or unhealthy ways, and our typical patterns of behaviour elicit clues about what we value most, and how we routinely get those needs met. This allows us to check our alignment and determine if the ways in which we are prioritising these needs, and how we are meeting them, are serving us well.

For example, I recently worked with a client for whom certainty was the highest priority. Out of a possible score of 140 on a questionnaire which assesses your preferences, she scored 130 for certainty. This is extremely high (and quite unusual). She freely acknowledged that she prioritised certainty whenever she was making a decision. This meant that she had created an extremely predictable and safe routine for herself.

She had worked in the same company for many years, attended the same gym for nearly as long, and did her shopping at the same time and place each week. Nothing wrong with any of that. Except for the fact that she felt extremely restless and unfulfilled in her life and wanted to meet new people. She was single and didn't want to be. The problem was, her need for certainty, which determined her schedule so rigidly, created almost no opportunities for her to cross paths with new people.

This is not to say that valuing certainty is always detrimental. However, an over-emphasis on this need, to the exclusion of the others, meant that my client's life felt one dimensional. She was safe, but bored. Assured, but unfulfilled, by her predictability. She loved knowing what was happening next, but also wondered about what else was possible. She was so tightly aligned to one value she was neglecting all of the others. By recognising her tendency to decide according to certainty first, she was able to introduce some alternatives, and become more intentional about meeting her own needs in a more balanced way.

3. Defining your version of success

One of the surest ways to feel dissatisfied with your life is to measure it against somebody else's definition of success. When you understand your personal values and your preferences in relation to the Six Universal Human Needs, you can more readily craft your own definition of success. The more clearly you can articulate what success looks like for you, the easier it is to assess your alignment. When you are out of alignment, objective measures of success don't resonate in the way you may expect them to, and you can find yourself saying things like, *"I should be happy, but..."*

This was the case for one of my clients, Tony, who presented with an intense but inscrutable sense of "blah". His reason for working with me was that he was looking to leave his current role and wanted to figure out what was next. However, when he described his job, I was initially confused. It sounded great. He had a high-ranking and well-paid position in a major corporation. He enjoyed respectful, even friendly, relationships with his colleagues, appreciated his supervisor's leadership style, and valued the inclusive and progressive culture of the organisation. On paper, he had no complaints.

So why did Tony want to leave? At first, he didn't know. He acknowledged that, on the surface, he had a great job, and he felt like he should love it. He just didn't. He felt underwhelmed and dissatisfied in his role. However, when he completed the values exercise and the Six Universal Human Needs questionnaire, the mystery of his dissatisfaction was solved.

Among Tony's top values were adventure and learning. His most emphasised need was growth, followed closely by variety. His thinking style was inherently big picture, and he was a natural leader, problem solver and innovator. He had a particular gift for anticipating the repercussions of minor changes and could pre-emptively address risks before they were realised.

Meanwhile, his job had him sitting in an office all day, every day. Although at a high level within the organisation, he was not in a leadership position. His responsibilities were primarily to implement policies, not create them. There was some capacity for problem solving, but the hierarchical nature of the organisation meant that he was often downstream of the actual issues. This meant that his capacity to create meaningful solutions was limited. Cue frustration, dissatisfaction and underwhelm.

So, despite the many ticks in the "pro" column of the equation, Tony's core values were not in alignment with his current role. He could objectively appreciate the many benefits to his position, but his inherent desire was to be challenged and in a diverse and adventurous environment. As such, it was not difficult to understand why sitting at a desk all day was failing to ignite his passion. His job was awesome. For someone else.

As Tony quickly discovered, the degree to which you are in alignment is likely to relate directly to the quality of your life. As such, I highly recommend investing some time into identifying your core values, your human needs preferences, and your definition of success. "Succeeding" in ways that don't align with your values is not conducive to maintaining your well-being and won't feel like success for very long.

Chapter 10

Set Intentions – Choose What You Want to BE and DO

"When your intentions are pure, so too will be your success."

Charles F. Glassman

BE first, DO second

Our daughter, Maddi, has always been strong-willed and articulate. When we first brought her home from hospital, we were astonished at how quickly she figured out what she wanted and how to get it. Within the first few hours of being home, our newborn managed to communicate in no uncertain terms that she preferred to be held, at all times, and if we had any aspirations whatsoever of her going to sleep, she would consider it on the basis that we played her favourite music and didn't put her anywhere near a cot. Her musical preference was initially the soundtrack from "Dances with Wolves," and then transitioned to Kenny Rogers. I kid you not. Clearly, we were newbie parents, clueless and scrambling. She had our measure, and she was not afraid of exerting her authority.

I realised very quickly that this parenting gig was a perfectionist's nightmare. All of the preparation we had done, the books we (actually I) had read, and the plans we had made, were rendered largely ineffectual by this small creature who dictated her own terms. I thought small babies slept a lot. Mine didn't. I thought they loved routines. Mine refused to comply with one. I thought I knew what to expect. I didn't. I thought I could do my PhD and care for a baby. Insert hysterical laughing here!

My intense awareness that my husband and I were solely responsible for the welfare of this child, and we couldn't afford to stuff it up, combined with my acute recognition that I had no idea what I was doing, meant that Naggy Nancy became a constant drone in my head. My need to be good was never more prominent than in those early years of parenthood, and it sucked a lot of the joy out of that special chapter in my life.

I remember being awed by how funny, clever, and cute she was, and wanting to press pause so she wouldn't grow up too quickly. At the same time, I was constantly looking for the definitive how-to-parent guide, as I felt completely out of my depth. The unpredictability of parenting pushed me out of my comfort zone, and I really wanted somebody to tell me how to do it.

One day when Maddi was about six, she asked me if she could have a chocolate. As we try to go with an "everything in moderation" approach, and she had already had some treats that day, I declined her request. She did not approve of my decision, and as is her custom, did not accept it. We discussed my decision at length. I explained how important it was to make good food choices, and that it was my job to help her to do that while she was still learning about nutrition. Her haughty response was: *"Well, I think you take your job too seriously."*

Touché. She didn't get the chocolate, but I had to concede that she was probably right. Just like in the early days when I despaired that she would ever go to sleep without the rigmarole of the ridiculous routine we had fallen prey to, there have been many occasions when I have stressed too much about the big picture implications of small stakes decisions.

Recognising my tendency to overthink and overinflate consequences of small decisions informed one of my most influential "being" aspirations. That is, to "be present". It sounds inconsequential, but it is powerful. When I am being present, I am able to make decisions based on the here and now, rather than from a position of the big picture or "what will this mean in five years' time?" perspective. It doesn't quite get me to a complete *laissez-faire* mindset, but it does lower the stakes and allow me to align with some of my other being aspirations: fun and flexible.

I acknowledge that I have often undervalued these attributes in favour of other values, such as working hard and achieving goals. Although this is not an inherently negative approach, and I am proud of some of those achievements, there have been times when more fun and flexibility, and less tenacity and determination, would have served me better and prevented a whole lot of drama.

Learn the lesson

In 2018, I completed my first marathon. The breathtaking scenery of Mt Cook in New Zealand was the backdrop, and I ticked a bucket list item when I crossed the finish line. However, in true perfectionist form, I wasn't satisfied. At around the 25km mark, my knee started to throb, and by the 30km mark, every step was agony. I completed the event, which was wonderful. But I didn't meet my target time, which was disappointing. Rather than celebrating my achievement, I began planning for my next marathon. Until I cracked that target time, I wasn't going to be satisfied. Talk about the fun police!

I chose the Sunshine Coast marathon, scheduled for August 2019 for my do-over. Training began in earnest in January 2019. I was fully committed. Together with a dear friend and training partner, I followed the training program to the second. I didn't miss a single session, and I didn't skimp on any of them. Throughout the entire campaign, I felt different to how I had felt the year before, but I didn't pay too much attention.

Every session felt hard, and I was more tired than I thought I would be. I rationalised that it was probably just my imagination and that I remembered the previous campaign with rose-coloured glasses. I reminded myself that it was supposed to be hard. Nobody trains for a marathon and says it is fun. Suck it up. Keep going. DON'T QUIT. You're a Witteveen, not a Quitterveen (a mantra Maddi coined ahead of her annual cross-country event in Year 1).

Apart from not feeling great, the lead up was objectively ideal. I met (and, in some cases, exceeded) my milestone challenges. In the days leading up to the event, I was diligent about monitoring my fluid intake, and I even got a massage two days prior. I stretched, foam rolled, rested, and ticked every box. On paper, I couldn't have been better prepared.

However, on the day, something went horribly wrong, and I collapsed with 300m to go. Yes, 300 miserly metres in a 42,200m event. I completed 99.29% of the marathon, and then I had absolutely nothing left. I hit a wall of darkness and ended up on the footpath, lapsing in and out of consciousness.

SET INTENTIONS – CHOOSE WHAT YOU WANT TO BE AND DO

My collapse was complete and devastating. In what seemed like a matter of seconds, I went from being on track for a PB, with the finish line clearly in my sights, to being on the ground, completely disoriented and incapable of moving myself out of the way or telling you my name. Upon investigation by the amazing medical team that assisted me, it became apparent that I was severely dehydrated, my temperature was dangerously high, and my blood sugar and blood pressure were dangerously low. In short, I was seriously ill, and the story could have had a vastly different ending if I had not received the excellent care that I did.

However, on reflection, it wasn't such a surprise. In addition to feeling lousy during training, I felt AWFUL during the run. My stats, as measured by my watch, were fine, but I didn't feel right. Other indicators, such as my temperature, were clearly off, but I wasn't paying attention to them. After about 10km, every step felt hard. By the halfway point, my running partner was looking at me with concern. Friends and family who were spectating could see that something was wrong, but I refused to acknowledge it. I kept pushing. I was committed.

My only focus was on that finish line, and I wasn't taking in the information that my body was sending me. I was unbelievably hot and couldn't regulate my temperature at all. Solution: pour water on my head and keep going. Blurred vision. Solution: Ignore it. Pounding in my skull. Solution: take no notice. I kept choosing to continue until the choice was taken away and I stepped into the abyss of unconsciousness.

During that run, I prioritised my doing goals over my being aspirations, and it cost me dearly. I focused so intently on the finish line that I wasn't present in the moment. This prevented me from taking in the clues that something was wrong, and I needed to make some adjustments. I showed zero aptitude for flexibility, and I can assure you I wasn't having any fun!

This situation also highlighted how far I had to go in my quest to break up with perfectionism, and my tendency to equate achievement with worthiness. Ouch.

When I was in the ambulance, covered in ice blankets and with ice packs jammed into and onto every square inch of available surface area across my body, three distinct and startling thoughts crystallised through the fog in my brain.

First, the complete disassociation from my body as I looked at all of the ice and couldn't feel any of it, made me wonder if I was dying. I felt so disconnected from my body and myself, for a few moments, I genuinely wondered if I was already dead.

The second thought was, "How could I do this to my family?". Even in that state of disorientation and confusion, I recognised that I had made choices that had not been in my favour. My next lucid thought was, "For f's sake, learn the lesson."

The great Carl Lewis once said, "*It's all about the journey, not the outcome.*" This is both true and incredibly hard to fully embrace when the outcome is not what you planned. It is somewhat easier to say you derived meaning from the process when it led to the desired outcome, than when things go awry.

But I knew there was a lesson to be learned from this experience. A big one. And it involved redefining success and failure and the importance of being more aligned to the process than the outcome. Just as Maddi had pointed out that I took my job as her nutritional gatekeeper too seriously, I had taken my self-imposed goal of getting a PB for that marathon too seriously.

In my quest to learn the lesson, derive the meaning, and move on from that experience, I found myself trying to identify the line between success and failure. If I considered my incomplete marathon to be a failure, at which point did I fail?

SET INTENTIONS – CHOOSE WHAT YOU WANT TO BE AND DO

Was it when I collapsed? Or was it when I focused so narrowly on my goal that I neglected the feedback I was receiving from my body? Was it when I failed to celebrate my successes along the way, and thus robbed myself of the pride and pleasure of committing to, and doing, hard things? Or perhaps when I chose to push through the physical pain rather than recalibrate and set a different goal?

In reality, it was none of those things, because I didn't actually fail. I set myself a big, audacious goal, and I achieved 99.29% of it. I committed to the process and pursued that unwaveringly. I did not complete the run, but I did everything I could to do so. My willpower was so strong, and my focus so complete, that I literally ran myself into oblivion.

Not that I recommend this, but I can see how pushing myself to the absolute limit could be a trait that has some benefits. On the flip side, if I had been more attuned to my being goals of being present, fun, and flexible, I could have potentially saved myself (and my loved ones) considerable anguish.

So, having decided that I didn't fail, I asked myself a different question: *How can I learn to redefine success in response to feedback?* I recognised that perhaps the lesson is about the need for agility and flexibility, rather than willpower alone. Considering a change in plan as pivoting, rather than quitting, gives permission for adjustments to be made without the burden of "failure".

As I was focusing my thoughts so carefully on the finish line, I neglected the signs my body was sending me that I needed to stop or, at the very least, slow down. I was so laser-focused on achieving my target time that I didn't allow myself a pivot – slowing down may have forfeited my time but would have potentially got me across the line. Knowing what I know now, would I exchange a slower time for a completed race? Absolutely!

My challenge for myself, and others, moving forward is this: when pursuing your doing goals, check in to see if they are still serving you. Are they aligned with your being goals, or do you need to pivot? Recalibrate? Reconsider? If so, I recommend you do it. It may be the vital ingredient that guarantees your success, whatever that means for you. I am continuing to work on my unhealthy attachment to achievement and being mindful of emphasising my *being* aspirations over my *doing* goals.

Chapter 11

Thankfulness – Make Gratitude Your Superpower

"Gratitude turns what we have into enough, and more. It turns denial into acceptance, chaos into order, confusion into clarity...it makes sense of our past, brings peace for today, and creates a vision for tomorrow."

Melody Beattie

Gratitude: a positive emotional response that we perceive on giving or receiving a benefit from someone[11].

---

[11] Emmons, R.A., and McCullough, M.E.(2004). *The Psychology of Gratitude (Series in Affective Science)*. New York: Oxford University Press.

An emerging body of empirical research has found support for the power of gratitude to influence psychological and physical well-being. A number of studies have found that consistent gratitude practices, such as daily gratitude lists or journaling, are associated with a range of positive outcomes, including increases in positive mood, subjective happiness, and life satisfaction, along with reductions in negative mood and depression symptoms[12]. Taken together, these findings provide compelling evidence for what we probably understand as an intuitive truth: being grateful is a powerful influencer of behaviour *and* it is good for you.

Not only do we feel good when we are expressing and experiencing gratitude, the research shows us that we are changing the way our brains operate and perceive the world. When we focus on positive things, this strengthens the neural pathways associated with positivity and makes us more likely to focus on positive things as a matter of routine, forming a reinforcing cognitive loop. In addition to benefits to individuals, gratitude offers social benefits, and has been associated with increasing prosocial behaviour, which enhances social relationships[13].

From this research, it is evident that gratitude has the capacity to do more than make you feel appreciation in the moment. Its impacts on your mood, cognition, and even brain structure and functioning, are significant and long-lasting. Personally, I have been aware of the benefits of gratitude for a long time, and I have been committed to enhancing my gratitude practice and that of my family. Each night at dinner we all share five things for which we are grateful (or, in the case of our youngest "what made me happy today"). This routine is a great way of

---

[12] Cunha, L.F., Pellanda, L.C., and Reppold, C.T. (2019). Positive psychology and gratitude interventions: A randomized clinical trial. *Frontiers in Psychology*, doi: 10.3389/fpsyg.2019.00584

[13] Allen, S. (2018) *The Science of Gratitude.* Berkeley: Greater Good Science Centre.

teaching our children to look for their blessings, and it gives us as parents an interesting insight into their worlds and what they are experiencing.

Unsurprisingly, with the critical mass of compelling scientific evidence in support of the benefits of gratitude, I've also been preaching on gratitude to my coaching clients. I encourage all of my clients to develop a gratitude practice as a way of enhancing their well-being and achieving greater clarity about what they truly value and appreciate. Those who do it report that it genuinely helps, which is why this has become a staple of my coaching practice.

But, I had an epiphany recently, and I'm a bit embarrassed at what I realised. Despite knowing all about the benefits of gratitude and encouraging those around me to develop a gratitude practice, I've been doing it wrong. When identifying the things for which I am grateful, I have focused exclusively on the things that I perceive to be positive AT THAT TIME.

In all of my gratitude practices, I had NEVER been grateful for something that was hard, hurtful, disappointing, or negative: at least, not at the time they were occurring. With the benefit of hindsight, I have been able to be grateful for difficult things that ultimately led to positive outcomes. But whilst the difficult thing remains difficult, there has been no gratitude from me WHATSOEVER.

This realisation got me thinking: if being grateful enhances well-being, and improves mood and quality of life, why do I wait for negative things to become positive before I am grateful? What would happen if I learned to be grateful for the hard things, when they are still hard? It seems possible that getting grateful sooner has the capacity to lessen the suffering and allow me to experience the benefits of gratitude before the situation has been resolved.

I recognise that I have become quite adept at finding and appreciating the lesson after the fact, but that seems like doing gratitude lip service. If I can assume (based on many examples) that it is safe to trust that the lesson is there, and I will find it, this opens up the possibility of being grateful in the moment – even before the lesson is clear. None of this is to suggest that gratitude is the antidote to all despair, or that simply being grateful will always be enough to make us feel better. Some things are genuinely awful, and it is naïve and unhelpful to suggest that we should always be grateful.

However, when I experience challenges which seem difficult and negative, I am endeavouring to cultivate gratitude in the moment, rather than waiting for the benefit of hindsight to highlight the opportunities presented by that situation. In so doing, I am optimistic that I will not only lessen my own (self-imposed) suffering, but also enhance my gratitude aptitude: both of which sound like a win to me!

The Total Truth Letter

When I was struggling to make peace with my decision to change my career, I felt many things. As I have previously shared, this represented something of an existential crisis for me and, as a result, I had a lot of mixed emotions to process. For many months, gratitude didn't make the list. I was stuck in a self-defeating loop, where I focused on what I had lost (a job that was no longer serving me, but in my mind = my career) and what I didn't know (what I was going to do next, but in my mind = who I was). Not much thankfulness to be found there!

One strategy that really helped me reframe that loop was the Total Truth Letter (credit to Sean Smith from Elite Coaching University for this exercise). This exercise is a powerful mechanism for working through emotions and getting resolution. It is based on the Hierarchy of Human Emotions, which proposes that the emotions attached to a difficult situation typically exist in a predictable hierarchy.

At the top of the hierarchy, which represents the most salient emotion, you find anger, followed by pain, fear, regret, and desire (what you wish was different). At the bottom of the hierarchy, representing the least salient emotion, is appreciation or gratitude. In the Total Truth Letter (which is not intended to be sent to any recipients) you address each of those emotions, in turn, expressing everything that you recognise as carrying that emotional energy. It is important that you follow the order of the hierarchy, and don't move on to the next one until the one before is complete.

When I worked up the courage to write my Total Truth Letter, I was genuinely surprised by what I wrote. As expected, I had a lot of colourful and highly charged emotions to express in my first paragraph, which encapsulated my anger. When I addressed the emotions in the middle of the hierarchy (pain, fear, regret, desire), I certainly had some things to say, but those sections were not nearly as voluminous or venomous as I had expected. The biggest and most perspective-shifting surprise came in the final section, when I dug deep to identify and acknowledge my appreciation and gratitude.

Despite my initial hesitation to begin that section, once I got going, words poured out of me, at a speed and intensity that shocked me. When I was finished, I had written more in the appreciation and gratitude section than in any of the others. I was stunned. From a chapter of my life that I would have described as one of my most challenging and difficult, emerged many things for which I was grateful. And not a superficial, Pollyanna-esque kind of grateful. I experienced a genuine, deeply felt, visceral recognition that I had actually benefited in many ways from that awful situation.

That exercise was extremely powerful for me. It showed me that good things really do come from adversity, but you have to make the effort to notice. If I hadn't stopped to capture my gratitude, not only would I not have acknowledged it, I wouldn't have received the benefits of it. Remembering and specifically naming those points of gratitude helped me to heal in ways that time and distance alone could not. Reminding myself of all I had gained, when it felt as though I had lost so much, was a catalyst for making peace with all that had transpired. This was a turning point in my journey, and one for which I am (you guessed it!) grateful.

Chapter 12

Undo – Undoing is Uncomfortable but Unavoidable

"The most difficult thing is the decision to act; the rest is merely tenacity."

Amelia Earhart

I invite you to stop and think about the last time you wanted to make a change in your life. A big one. One that you knew would be really good for you, and you would be so proud of yourself if you did it. The benefits may have included better health, well-being, fitness, relationships, or feelings of satisfaction and/or accomplishment.

Now think about the excuses you made that ensured you didn't follow through completely. I could be wrong, but I'm guessing they were plausible enough to justify not fully implementing the change you wanted to make. Those excuses might have included variations of:

I'm too busy.

I don't have time.

I'm too tired.

I just can't fit another thing in right now.

I don't have the headspace.

I don't have the energy.

I can't afford it...

These excuses are all examples of limiting beliefs and are a great place to start when we are looking for what we need to undo in order to be successful. Although it may seem counterintuitive, one of the most helpful strategies I have found for implementing change is to start by figuring out what I can undo, stop doing, or take out of my life, before I try to add anything new. This can be important from a logistical perspective, i.e., to create more time to do something new, but it can be even more vital from a mindset perspective.

Some of my most powerful shifts have come from undoing detrimental thought and behavioural habits that reinforced my feelings of needing to be good, inadequacy and stuckness. These have included (among many others!): negative self-talk, putting too much pressure on myself, and overthinking *every* element of *every* step of *every* process of *every* aspect of anything I am attempting for the first time. I have also found myself getting caught in the myth that busyness is a sign of progress and success. Allowing myself to stop and BE in the midst of busyness can provide a much greater return on investment than constantly striving to get things done.

When thinking about what you may want to undo in order to create space for more positive and empowering ways of being, it is helpful to remember that whilst learning a new skill is hard, changing the way you think and feel can be much harder. Through the amazing power of neuroplasticity, our brains continue to create myelin throughout our lives, meaning that we can learn and improve on many things, right through to older adulthood. However, we can't undo the myelin we have developed. It decays and breaks down through age and illness, but once developed, it stays in place. The only way to create alternate pathways in the brain is to myelinate different pathways by practising other ways of being[14].

This means that implementing meaningful and lasting change takes time and repetition. If you recognise a thought or behavioural pattern you wish to change, research suggests it takes between 18 and 254 days, with an average of 66 days for the new behaviour to become automatic.[15] In addition to allowing for time and practice, Charles Duhigg, author of "The Power of Habit," identified that to successfully change a habit you need to:

1. Identify an alternative to replace your old habit (rather than just deciding you want to stop doing something – what do you want to do instead?);

2. Have a good understanding of why you want to change your habit; and

3. Believe that change is possible.

---

[14] Coyle, D. (2010). *The Talent Code: Greatness isn't born, it's grown.* Great Britain: Cornerstone.

[15] Lally, P., van Jaarsveld, H.M., Potts, H.W.W., and Wardle, J. (2009). How are habits formed: Modelling habit formation in the real world. *European Journal of Social Psychology*, doi: 10.1002/ejsp.674

WHY BEING GOOD CAN BE BAD FOR YOU

When I was a kid, my favourite sport was netball. I started when I was 8 and played every season until I finished school. When I was about 12 or 13, some of the players from the Queensland team facilitated a training session for regional and rural kids in a nearby city. I was so excited to attend and couldn't wait to learn from such a distinguished group of players. After the generic skills and drills session, the group was split into shooters, defenders, and mid-court players for specialised coaching. I went with the shooters.

My natural tendency in new situations is to sit back and watch what happens, so I can assess how things work and what I need to do to fit in. You can imagine my alarm when the coach called on me to be the first of the attendees to demonstrate their shooting prowess to our celebrity trainers. With sweaty palms and a strong inkling that I may in fact vomit, I took my first shot. To my tremendous relief, it went in. So did the next two. With three in a row, I began to relax. There was nothing to worry about.

After my third shot, the coach came over to me and kindly but firmly told me I needed to adjust my style. I was surprised and deflated. I had just shot three in a row! She went on to explain that although I was undoubtedly accurate, I was holding the ball quite low at the point of release, thus making my shot easier to defend, especially for a tall defender. After demonstrating the preferred shooting style, she moved on to the next player, leaving me to practise my new shooting style.

In the weeks that followed, I diligently practised the new shooting style. I had a goal post at home, and I would go downstairs each afternoon, earnestly trying to recreate the flawless high-release style I had been shown. For all of my eagerness and willingness to learn and adapt, I couldn't get it right. I tried so hard, but it felt awkward and weird. I had been playing netball for about five years at this stage, so my old style was fairly entrenched in my muscle memory.

After a few frustrating weeks, I gave up. I decided that it was too hard, and I wasn't going to bother trying to change my style. To really consolidate my decision, I worked myself into a state of righteous indignation, by focusing on the fact that I was already an accurate shooter, so there was no need to bother with this new approach. The line was drawn in the sand – I was retreating back to how things were. I had no idea who to credit with the adage of, "If it ain't broke, don't fix it," but I agreed with them. I felt fully justified in my decision to revert back to my old style.

The problem was, I couldn't do it anymore. The ease of my old style was completely elusive. I tried everything. I tried being deliberate, consciously focusing on undoing each element of the new style I had been taught and replacing it with how I used to do it, working my way up from my feet to my fingers. I tried being spontaneous, simply grabbing the ball and shooting quickly before I could overthink it. I tried closing my eyes. Walking away and coming back to start fresh. All to no avail. I was in netball shooting purgatory. I had unlearned my old style but hadn't learned the new one sufficiently to replace it. Whether I tried the old or the new, I got awkward. And rebounds.

This experience is not uncommon. I have heard similar stories of people who taught themselves to play golf, and then got lessons, and had to unlearn and relearn every element of their golf swing. It is almost enough to make you quit the game altogether. When we have done things a certain way for a long time, it is hard to do them differently. We can understand what to do, how to do it, and why it is a good idea, but it can still be difficult to implement the change. The temptation can be strong to just go back to the way things were.

However, just as you can't unknow or unsee something, often you can't undo a change that has begun the implementation process. Once you have committed to the change, navigating the no-man's land between the old and the new can be difficult, and you may feel like giving up. However, as we have previously discussed, sometimes you have to burn the boats and go all in.

My secret weapon: The simple reframe

When you are breaking up with being good, you may recognise the value of undoing some of your expectations or reprogramming some of your internal narratives. It may be a challenge to mute your version of Naggy Nancy, but it is worth persisting. One of the best techniques I have found for changing thoughts or interpretations that are negative or self-defeating is the reframe. In its simplest form, the reframe is an alternative perspective or interpretation of an event or situation that is more positive or empowering than the original.

For example, one of my clients shared with me how guilty she felt when she went to the gym early in the morning because she liked to be there when her kids woke up. Despite acknowledging that there was no harm being done to her kids (her husband was there to take care of them), my client still felt guilty. We then discussed the benefits she derived from going to the gym. Although she listed several, including having more energy, a clearer head, and feeling calmer after exercising, those benefits weren't enough to abate her feelings of guilt.

When I asked her what benefits her kids derived from her going to the gym, she looked confused, then thoughtful, and then she beamed. "They get a Mum who feels energetic and positive because she feels great after going to the gym." Bingo. There's the reframe – instead of focusing on what her kids were missing out on, we considered what her kids were getting, and this changed her perspective entirely.

Allowing herself to recognise that taking care of herself wasn't selfish, and certainly wasn't detrimental to her children, meant that my client not only gave herself permission to go to the gym, she committed to doing so – for her own sake, and for her kids. In this way, asking yourself a different question can be an effective reframe and a way of liberating yourself from unrealistic expectations.

Undoing the need for perfectionism in a pandemic

The year 2020 will undoubtedly go down in the history books as one of the most tumultuous, uncertain, and chaotic times ever documented. In the climate of uncertainty and confusion created by the COVID-19 pandemic, many of us were thrust unceremoniously into a state of chaos. For some, the realities of COVID-19 meant extreme physical and/or mental health risks; for others, the risks were economic; for many, it was both.

In addition, there are the very real the challenges associated with social disruption on a global scale, where people across the globe are required to be physically distant from most, if not all, of their support network. With the widespread cancellation of almost every "non-essential" activity, it is totally understandable for people to feel lost, isolated, and afraid.

The early months of the pandemic were a time of undoing on a global scale. Almost all of us were required to let go of many of our expectations about how things "had" to be and reconfigure almost every facet of our lives. Unsurprisingly, disruption on this scale reverberated through every household, and created many difficulties.

For many of my clients the changes imposed as a result of the pandemic created tremendous stress, angst, and uncertainty. However, as time went on, many found themselves a rhythm or routine which, although not ideal and for many, not preferable, wasn't all negative either. One of the key differentiators between those who adapted and those who did not appeared to be the willingness to surrender expectations.

We have been extremely fortunate that our home state has had relatively few cases of COVID-19, and as a result, the restrictions we experienced were minimal and insignificant compared to many other areas. However, even with that caveat, the uncertainty surrounding the trajectory of this pandemic, together with the experience of temporary restrictions, required me to undo many of my expectations also.

After having many conversations with clients across the country, who were enduring varying levels of restrictions, I recognised that there may be some benefits in sharing my experience. Adjusting to the pandemic felt like one big continuous undoing, with multiple reframes built in. I wrote myself a letter to capture this experience and have previously shared it as a blog. I share it here also, as I think it provides a good example of the benefits of undoing and the role the reframe can play in that process.

Dear Pre-Pandemic Me,

You are not going to believe what is coming. It is going to be one of those defining moments in history that your grandchildren and subsequent generations will learn about at school. As hard as it is to wrap your brain around, this is the absolute truth: a pandemic is coming, and it will result in large-scale shutdowns across the globe.

Schools, businesses, shops, even beaches and parks, are going to be shut, and people will be required to stay at home, to the greatest extent possible. Laws will be invoked that mean you can get fined or even jailed for travelling too far away from home, being in a public place unnecessarily, and even eating a kebab on a park bench. Many will suffer terribly, and the global health and economic costs will be unfathomable. I know, it's unbelievable, but the history books will back me up.

UNDO – UNDOING IS UNCOMFORTABLE BUT UNAVOIDABLE

One of the things I want you to know about this crazy time is that it will seem surreal for a while. There will be a sense of imminent (albeit vague and somewhat removed) danger, and whilst individual responses will differ, most people with whom you interact will be experiencing some type of elevated emotion, ranging from mild concern to near panic. This includes the children, who will initially experience this pandemic as a thief of joy.

They will be upset when they realise they cannot go to school, participate in their extra-curricular activities, visit their family, or play with their friends. They will be horrified to discover that even simple pleasures like playing in the playground or going to the beach are forbidden. Two out of the three will have "isolation birthdays," where there is no party, no friends, no extended family visiting. Presents will be relatively scarce, with "IOUs" or cash transfers the most likely gifts they will receive. School camps and sports carnivals will be cancelled. Most of the things they look forward to will be off-limits, and they will grieve.

Although it may be tempting to dismiss these as small and trivial problems, they are big and meaningful to these kids. Be kind to them. Their lives have never been so disrupted and it will take some time for them to adjust. Just like typical grief, it won't be linear. They will have good days, and then they will re-experience a surge of emotion as the reality of the situation is reinforced in another way.

It may be the reality of their upcoming birthday, or the passing of a date on which something special that was on the calendar is no longer a thing. It may be the crushing disappointment of realising that they can't visit their baby cousin on his first birthday, or simply seeing the sign on the swings at the park that says, "Closed".

After the initial surrealness will come the frustration, as it becomes apparent exactly how difficult it can be to keep everyone entertained, occupied, fed, and on speaking terms when nobody leaves the house AT ALL. Working from home whilst supervising kids' learning will become the challenge which most parents undertake, with varying degrees of confidence and enthusiasm.

WHY BEING GOOD CAN BE BAD FOR YOU

Even with the best of intentions and the most wholehearted attempts, you will find that it is HARD to be productive, effective, patient and kind when you are juggling so many things and don't get a chance to think your own thoughts without being interrupted. You will remind yourself of your blessings and the fact that many others are doing it way tougher than you, and this will be true. It will also do little to make it easier to do what you need to do in the way you hope to do it.

You will feel many emotions: fear, uncertainty, frustration, despair, anger, and guilt (so much guilt!). However, you will learn, grow, and adapt as well. There will be opportunities to reflect, connect, and clarify what is most important. In this clarification, you will have the opportunity to re-evaluate your priorities and rediscover what REALLY matters. In this, you will have an unprecedented opportunity to become crystal clear about your blessings and the things that truly add value to your life, and equally, what you can do without.

You will realise that many of the things which felt like time-consuming irritations, like the multitude of extra-curricular activities that you spend so much time dropping off to and picking up from, are precious opportunities for each of your family members to belong, participate, and connect with others.

The sadness you will feel when events that felt like mere obligations, like cross-country carnivals and the commencement of the footy season are cancelled, will highlight how important those events were to the kids and even to you. The longing you will feel to visit with your family, hug your nieces and nephews, and chat with your mum, your siblings, and your friends, will remind you how blessed you are to have those people in your life. The way you wish you could just go to, well, anywhere, will show you how fortunate you are to have the freedom you enjoy.

You will innovate. They say that necessity is the mother of invention, and this is true. You will create and participate in neighbourhood scavenger hunts, design PE lessons, have Nerf gun battles, engage in craft activities, and find ways to tempt an unwilling five-year-old into learning sight words (hint - chalk on the driveway + waterbombs was the winner).

You will request and receive video and written submissions from family across the country, sending birthday wishes to your now teenage daughter. You will mastermind a surprise Zoom party for your son, and secretly arrange for his class to sing "Happy Birthday" to him in their virtual classroom. You will create new birthday traditions which result in both of them declaring their isolation birthdays one of the best yet.

You will lower your own unrealistic expectations of yourself, and accept that, on some days, just maintaining a relative level of peace and calm is an achievement. Sometimes, you will rejoice in the simplicity; on other days you will be stifled by the monotony. You will support others to accept these fluctuations as normal, and you will allow yourself to accept them too. Your clients will need you to be calm, and you will help them to adjust. In so doing, you will adjust also.

You will run. A lot. More than you have ever run before. Sometimes because you joined a challenge and wanted to complete it; sometimes because you need to get out of the house REALLY badly; and sometimes because you are remembering how good it feels to be run-fit again, after a period of poor health. Your speed and endurance will improve, and you will feel a sense of satisfaction that perhaps your best times aren't necessarily behind you, despite the close proximity of a significant birthday.

Your kids will watch an exorbitant amount of Netflix, and you will too. Screen time usage will be at an all-time high, and you will occasionally panic about this. However, you will remember that this is not your new forever normal. It is a strange and temporary situation which will have little to no bearing on how your household consumes media in the weeks and months to come. When other options are available for entertainment, screens will return to the back burner.

Speaking of screens, you will spend an inordinate amount of time looking at your screen for work also. You will serve your clients via Zoom, which you will find draining, but recognise that it is better than the alternative, which is to not serve them at all. You will enjoy some of the innovative ways others are making use of the online world, and you will also feel *overwhelmed by the sheer volume of information coming at you online. Create boundaries for media consumption and don't fall into the trap of reading everything there is to read about the pandemic. Stay informed enough to stay safe, but trust that you don't need to read it all.*

You will long for the return to normal, but you will acknowledge that a complete return to normal is not ideal. There will be elements of lockdown that you will want to keep. Movie nights, board games, and family bike rides will become regular rather than sometimes activities. You will recognise the gift of being less busy and the creativity that was sparked by the yawning gaps in the family's schedule which have never before existed. You will appreciate the exercise habits that each member of the family has developed, and you will encourage them all to keep them up.

Overall, I want you to know that this time will be crazy and hard, but it will be rich with unexpected blessings, particularly in relation to recognising what really matters. Don't waste it, and don't rush too quickly back to 'normal'. Take the opportunity to design your new normal, taking the best bits from isolation and merging them with the best bits of freedom to connect with people and participate in activities that bring joy and add value to your life.

XX Mid-Pandemic Me

PS There will be many opportunities for questionable online purchasing decisions. Trust me on this: you don't need those jeans. Oh, and "M&Ms" are not actually an empirically supported antidote to homeschool stress, despite what you may tell yourself.

Although not limited to the realm of undoing, the reframe offers a powerful addition to the arsenal for habit change. It is an effective mechanism for generating alternative options that you want to use instead of your ways of thinking, feeling, and behaving that aren't serving you well. So, when you accept the time and repetition that is required, use the reframe to create alternatives, remember why you want to make the change (clues will be found in the Align and Set Intentions sections of the framework), and believe that you can make the change; you will be using scientifically validated techniques to change your habits in ways that are powerful and meaningful to you.

Chapter 13

Together – Your People Make Hard Times Easier and Good Times Better

---

"Sometimes, reaching out and taking someone's hand is the beginning of a journey. At other times, it is allowing another to take yours."

Vera Nazarian

When I was developing the ASTUTE framework, including the element of togetherness was a no-brainer. However, this has been the hardest chapter to write in this book. Part of the challenge has been the many and different ways in which togetherness is important. The multitude of research findings that support our need for connection, the impact of our social environment on our outcomes, and my personal experiences of the importance of having good people in my corner, are plentiful enough for another book entirely. Also, it seems self-evident, and therefore possibly redundant for me to emphasise the fact that we are more likely to thrive when we are connected to the right people.

We know from the Harvard Study of Adult Development, an extraordinary longitudinal study which commenced in 1938 and continues to the current day, that one of the most important predictors of happiness and longevity is meaningful human connections[16]. This suggests that even the most introverted among us do better when we have quality connections with others.

It is worth noting the difference between *quality* and *quantity* of relationship, with the Harvard Study of Adult Development finding that it is specifically the quality of connections that bestows the benefits. As I reflect on my journey thus far, the importance of connection is abundantly evident, and never more apparent than during times of change in the toughest of circumstances.

Take action and you will find your people

> "When the student is ready, the teacher will appear."
>
> **Unknown, but often incorrectly attributed to Buddha**

On the day I decided to leave my career, I signed up for a coaching qualification. And then another, a few weeks later. And then two more. Within the first 12 months, I think I completed six qualifications. I was a course junkie. In reality, I was frantically trying to stifle my fear of the unknown by filling the void with credentials, because that felt safe and familiar.

---

[16] Mineo, L. (2017). Good genes are nice, but joy is better. *Harvard Gazette*, www.news.harvard.edu/gazette

I hoped that if I added more qualifications to my CV, I would feel less like a fraud. I acknowledge that completing so many in such a short space of time was excessive. However, there was an unexpected bonus that emerged from my newfound course addiction, and it helped me tremendously as I navigated the uncharted territory of my life beyond academia.

It wasn't the qualifications that helped me to transition to my new life. It was the people I met along the way. By signing up to those courses, I expanded my social and professional circle, and it was amazing. I connected with other coaches, entrepreneurs, and business owners, all at different stages on their journey. They inspired, encouraged, and educated me. They made it ok not to know what I was doing, and they celebrated my successes.

Research has demonstrated that our social environment impacts on many facets of life, in ways that may be surprising. The concept of "social contagion," whereby individuals behave in ways that align with their immediate social group and get similar outcomes, has been empirically supported in many studies.[17] This suggests that who we associate with can dramatically influence our quality of life and our capacity to achieve our goals.

The best example of the power of a like-minded community occurred when I signed up to be certified in Conversational Intelligence®. As part of that program, I was assigned a peer group. That group had members from across the United States, New Zealand, and Australia. We met monthly via Zoom for six months, and within that time, we met with most of the group individually at least once.

The depth of connection that was forged within that group was as unexpected as it was welcome. Over a year after our

---

[17] Burchard, B. (2017). *High Performance Habits*. Carlsbad: Hay House.

certification course was completed, we continue to meet. Our meetings are no longer mandated for our course requirements. We choose to meet to support one another and share in each other's journeys. These relationships have sustained me in my business journey, as those ladies are fellow coaches and business owners who understand the challenges and celebrate the wins. This type of connection is different from the personal connections of friends and family, but it is no less important to success.

Having others who understand your journey is invaluable, especially when you are trying something new. If you are looking to make a change in your life, I highly recommend finding those who have already done it, or are thinking about it, and make a connection. There is something magical about talking with someone who says, "I totally get it,", and they totally mean it. I went looking for qualifications and found people, and that was much better.

The paradox of loss and connection

Sometimes you may need to find new people to accompany you on your journey. At other times, you need to cherish the ones you already have. This was never truer for me than when my third pregnancy began as a twin pregnancy and finished as a single pregnancy. One of my twins miscarried early in the pregnancy, and I was presented with the greatest paradox I have ever encountered – how to grieve the loss of one child, whilst preparing to celebrate the birth of another.

Losing one of my twins created a terrible bind for me. I wanted to mourn her loss and grieve for her. However, I still had a healthy baby growing inside of me, whom I needed to protect from my overwhelming emotion. I also had two healthy children who needed me to be ok. I knew that stress was bad for babies in utero, so I didn't want to be stressed. I shut down emotionally and thought I was coping.

There were clues that I wasn't, like the tears on my pillow when I woke in the morning, the constant headache I endured for the duration of my pregnancy, and the way that my excitement about Hugo's impending birth was muted and lacked enthusiasm. Yet, I persisted with my numbness. In an effort to protect Hugo, myself, and my family from big emotions, I turned inward. I withdrew emotionally from almost everyone. I was so focused on being strong and brave, I lost sight of the fact that I didn't have to be alone.

I was brutally aware that I wasn't "as pregnant" anymore. I had one healthy baby, for which I was grateful. But I had lost a baby, for which I was devastated. The looming pain was so overwhelming, I was afraid to let myself feel it. Connected to the pain of loss were guilt and fear. Guilt that I had somehow caused my baby's inability to grow and flourish. Fear that whatever had happened to cause that loss would happen again.

We all hold a deep fear that we are not enough. In this situation, my deepest fear was that I wasn't enough for my baby. I couldn't nurture her enough, so she could grow and come into the world with her brother. I couldn't provide the nourishment and the healthy environment for her to flourish. I wanted to experience and express my feelings of guilt and anger and so much sadness, but I was afraid of what would happen if I indulged in these emotions.

I didn't know who to talk to about this situation, as it is an unusual type of loss. I didn't want to overwhelm my husband with my pain. He had his own to carry. Same with my mum. I couldn't talk about this with other parents who have experienced pregnancy loss. It seems insensitive when you still have a healthy child from this pregnancy. Similarly, I couldn't talk about this with other parents who have not experienced pregnancy loss. It would make them feel uncomfortable. My need to be good dictated the importance of not causing a fuss. So, my approach was: don't talk about it; don't think about it; but most of all, don't feel about it.

When the pain threatened to break through my armour, I would try to rationalise it away. I would tell myself that it was better that there was only one, as it would be easier physically, emotionally, psychologically, financially. We didn't plan for twins, so it was like nothing had changed. Except it had. The knowledge that there were two, if only for a short time, changed everything. Knowing she existed made me love her. Losing her without ever meeting her was a loss I felt I couldn't endure.

Not allowing myself to feel the pain, the guilt, the fear, and the anger seemed like the sensible approach. However, numbness doesn't discriminate. For every negative emotion I was inoculating myself against, there was a positive emotion I was missing out on. Being numb robbed me of the feelings of joy, anticipation, curiosity, and expectation about Hugo. I didn't want to imagine what he would be like, because I would automatically imagine what his sister would have been like. I struggled to see him separately from his sister. Every milestone of his was inextricably linked with the milestone his sister didn't get to achieve.

I knew that living without feeling was not healthy. Neither was suffering alone. Over time, I came to recognise that I had to let myself feel, if only so that awful headache would dissipate. I had to acknowledge the pain, guilt, fear, and anger so I could get to the good stuff. I had to acknowledge my intense feelings of loss, so I could access my intense feelings of gratitude.

I also had to reconnect with my loved ones. My husband was suffering also. I had tried to spare him the depth of my anguish, as I didn't want to add to his. But the silo approach wasn't working, so I gave myself permission to feel the pain, even though I was afraid that it might break me.

My turning point came when I let my emotional walls down and let my mum in. Sharing my grief, and allowing her to sit in it with me, was healing. It also reminded me of the love and support I had all around me, and the fact that I didn't have to bear the burden in isolation. Soon after I accepted the comfort my mum had been offering for so long, I had a dream.

It was one of the most vivid dreams I have ever had, and it brought me the first sense of peace I felt since I had lost my twin. In my dream, there were hands. They were big, strong, trustworthy hands. And they were familiar. They were my dad's hands. In his hand, lay my lost baby. She was safe, and she was loved.

I woke with tears streaming down my face, and I felt grateful. That dream had given me a sense of hope that my dad and my baby were together, and that thought sustained me. Eventually, I was able to feel the joy and to recognise that Hugo is a gift in his own right. He is not defined by his missing twin. My love for him is strong and uncomplicated. I no longer saw him as half of an incomplete whole. He brings joy and happiness. He amplifies emotions. He lives large, and I allow myself to think he lives for two. It is no coincidence that my healing came through connection. It always does.

The lesson I learned from this difficult chapter wasn't new. I had just forgotten it temporarily. In my quest to be good and strong and brave and stoic, I retreated and disconnected from my loved ones. Despite my best intentions, that didn't protect anyone, and it certainly didn't allow me to process my grief in any way. The peace came when I reconnected, and when my subconscious allowed me the gift of sensing a connection between my two lost loves. I have no way of knowing where that image came from, but it symbolises connection in the deepest and purest form, and it continues to sustain me to this day.

Connection: It's for everybody

Whether we profess to be "people people" or not, our need for connection is fundamental and hard-wired. A substantial body of research has demonstrated that our brains experience social pain (i.e., rejection) in the same circuits as physical pain[18]. This body of research helps to explain why social isolation can be so detrimental, even when we are more digitally connected than ever before.

One of the resounding lessons from the COVID-19 pandemic has been that, although we can find innovative ways of connecting in times of social isolation, technology remains a poor substitute for actually being in a room with others. This is not to undermine the powerful connections that can be made online, but most would agree that there is a qualitative difference in our ability to connect meaningfully in a purely online environment, compared to in person. So, physical proximity appears important when it comes to meaningful connections.

However, proximity alone is not enough for meaningful connection. In my first semester of university, I was surrounded by tens of thousands of students, and felt utterly alone. As a country kid living in the city for the first time, I felt invisible and intimidated by the sheer number of people with whom I came into contact on a daily basis. I was keenly aware of the complete lack of meaningful connection in the midst of that mass of humanity.

---

[18] Eisenberger, N.I. (2012). Broken hearts and broken bones: A neural perspective on the similarities between social and physical pain. *Current Directions in Psychological Science.* https://doi.or/10.1177/0963721411429455

TOGETHER – YOUR PEOPLE MAKE HARD TIMES EASIER

The great thing is, we are all capable of creating meaningful connection in even the most fleeting of exchanges. Simply making eye contact can be enough to make a connection that tells the other person they matter. Whether you are talking to your child, loved one, friend, colleague, or the barista at your local coffee shop, giving them your full attention in that moment can create a sense of belonging and connection.

Surrounding yourself with people who support you, cheer for you, commiserate with you, teach you, learn from you, and appreciate you, is a vital element of success, however you define it. It is worth considering:

Who are your people?

Who else do you want on your team?

Who is currently on your team but don't deserve their spot?

Who do you serve?

Who is serving you?

Who teaches you?

Who do you teach?

Who do you have fun with?

Who challenges you to be your best?

Who is setting an example to which you aspire?

Who are you setting an example for?

It is evident that great things tend to happen through connection, rather than isolation. Even solo pursuits that can be accomplished alone tend to be made easier or more enjoyable if others are involved in some meaningful way. And this doesn't just apply to the extroverts. As a confirmed introvert, who is highly self-directed and autonomous, I can attest to the importance of finding the right people to have in your corner. However, out of allegiance to my fellow introverts, I must emphasise the importance of not having too many of them in your space at the same time. Too much peopling is exhausting!

Chapter 14

Elevate – Thank Yourself Later

"Focus on progress not perfection."

Bill Phillips

One of the defining principles of Gestalt psychology is that the whole is greater than the sum of its parts. Consistent with this principle is the idea that making small, incremental changes will improve your outcomes exponentially. This is the basis of the Elevate component of the ASTUTE Transformation Framework.

Whilst the earlier components are relatively introspective and reflective, the Elevate phase is about implementation. It is about identifying and implementing actions that will align with your aspirations, so you can begin to progress towards your desired outcomes. It is also about cultivating a mindset of continuous improvement and optimism.

As described in the framework overview, the guiding question of the Elevate component of the model is: *"What can I do today that I will thank myself for tomorrow?"* The beauty of this approach is that it provides scope for you to choose something small but meaningful to implement. When you create a critical mass of small changes, you are likely to begin to feel more widespread benefits. The ultimate goal is to elevate your life by enhancing all facets that are meaningful to you. In this chapter, I will describe the simple process I have been implementing since I left my career and became my own first client.

1. Conduct a life and well-being check

A helpful exercise in this regard is the "Wheel of Life"[19] (a full explanation and template for this exercise is available in the companion guide). In this exercise, you simply give yourself a current rating of satisfaction in a range of life dimensions, together with your ideal rating. You then identify actions you can take in each dimension to close the gap between your current and ideal ratings. Having identified what matters most to you and where you want to improve, the next logical step is to create a plan to "up-level" in each area. This phase will be informed by what you have identified throughout the other components of the ASTUTE framework. The most important thing is to choose actionable steps which you can implement readily.

In psychology, there is a principle of perception known as the "just noticeable difference" (JND). This relates to the threshold or tipping point at which a stimulus becomes detectable. For example, the amount of perfume that needs to be sprayed

---

[19] Paul J. Meyer, founder of Success Motivation Institute® is credited with creating this concept, which is commonly used in the coaching industry.

into a room before it is noticed can be measured as the JND. When applying this concept to goal setting, the idea is to choose something small enough that you are able to do it, but big enough that you will notice the benefits of doing so. If our up-levelling activity is too insignificant, we are likely to stop bothering with it. If it is too difficult, same result. Aim for something in between – easy enough to implement; big enough to detect a change.

2. Be constantly curious

The way you choose to elevate your life is entirely personal and will be unique to you. For me, the biggest contributor to my personal development has been my dedication to continuous learning. I am constantly curious, and actively seek out new information on a range of topics as often as I can.

I have always been an avid reader, and I used to gravitate towards historical fiction and crime thrillers. Whilst I still enjoy curling up with a novel as a form of relaxation, in recent times, I have become much more intentional about reading books which teach me something. I am fortunate to be a fast reader, which enables me to consume large quantities of information in a relatively short time.

I love reading so much that when I was initially trying to figure out what to do with myself when I left academia, I toyed with the idea of creating executive summaries of the most interesting books I had read and sharing them with others who don't read as quickly as I do. You can imagine my disappointment when I discovered that my great idea was already a thing. (Blinkist, I'm looking at you!)

So, although that turned out not to be my million dollar idea, my love of reading is a significant contributor to my version of elevating my life. I have also become a podcast junkie and take advantage of the many hours in which "Mum's taxi" is in operation to listen to educational podcasts. There is an abundance of helpful information available, and I find tremendous benefit in taking advantage of it.

3. Choose something to implement

You may have heard the adage, "information doesn't equal transformation," which is absolutely true. For information to facilitate a transformation, it needs to go through two additional steps: personalisation and implementation. This means that you not only source the information, you actively apply it to your personal situation, and create a goal to implement something that you have learned.

However, setting goals does not guarantee we will achieve them. It has been estimated that approximately 80% of New Year's resolutions fail by February[20]. Although the empirical basis of that estimate is difficult to establish, anecdotal and personal experience support the fact that those who achieve their New Year's resolutions are the exceptions rather than the rule.

I can certainly relate to this phenomenon of making solemn and sincere declarations of intent about how I'm going to do better in the coming year on 1 January, starting off with a bang, and then forgetting what I even vowed to do a few weeks later. Whilst various explanations have been offered to account for this high attrition rate, the common themes converge around the goals being overly ambitious, vague, and/or not very compelling. The biggest behavioural predictor of failure is a lack of consistent implementation.

---

[20] Luciani, J. (2015). Why 80 percent of New Year's resolutions fail. *US News & Health Report*, www.health.usnews.com/health-news.

Whilst it is relatively simple to adjust the goals so they are less likely to end up on the discard pile, finding a way to facilitate consistent implementation is more difficult. As we have already identified, one of the necessary (but not sufficient) elements of successful habit (re)formation is a belief that change is possible. For me, this constitutes a success mindset.

If you search the personal development or self-help aisle in any bookstore, you will find a myriad of formulae and models that outline the components of a success mindset. After reading many of them, it became apparent that, although the language and precise configurations differ, those that were based on research shared some common elements. Those key elements can be summarised in a simple conceptual overview: Grit, Growth and Gratitude.

Synonymous with the work of Angela Duckworth, *grit* can be defined as "passion and perseverance"[21]. Grit is evidenced by continuing to work towards goals, even when they feel difficult or out of reach. The concept of a *growth mindset* is most commonly attributed to the work of Carol Dweck[22] and refers to the benefit of believing that change is possible. Like grit, the concept of a growth mindset was initially developed in the context of academic achievement.

However, both have broader applicability. In a more general sense, these two constructs speak to the importance of persisting through adversity, recognising that failing is part of learning, and actively seeking to incorporate the lessons from the failures in order to get closer to our goals. The idea of failing forward is well aligned with these principles.

---

[21] Duckworth, A. (2016). *Grit: The Power of Passion and Perseverance*. New York: Simon & Schuster.
[22] Dweck, C.S. (2008). *Mindset: The New Psychology of Success*. New York: Ballantine Books.

I recently listened to an interview with Sara Blakely, Founder of Spanx. At the time she became a billionaire, she was the youngest female self-made billionaire in history. Although there were numerous factors that went into Sara's phenomenal success, and she epitomises many characteristics of successful people, her incredible capacity for failing stood out to me.

When she was growing up, Sara's father would ask her each day how she had failed that day. This encouraged her to actively seek out opportunities and circumstances which made her uncomfortable. The beauty of this approach was that it took the fear out of failing. Failing was the goal, not something to be avoided. By routinely looking for opportunities to fail, Sara trained herself to take risks and push herself in ways that those who fear failure would never do. This represents the ultimate success mindset.

The final component of the success mindset, namely *gratitude*, has been discussed at length in Chapter 11. As a reminder, when we focus on what we are grateful for, we enhance our mood, well-being, and outlook, which, in turn, increases the likelihood that we will take action. Motivation and momentum create a reinforcing loop, whereby you feel motivated when you have momentum, which in turn, enhances motivation. As such, actively cultivating these three components of a success mindset provides a solid foundation upon which to implement change and achieve your goals.

In describing the ASTUTE Transformation Framework, my intention has been to provide a series of complementary strategies that are easy to implement and will facilitate meaningful change. I have integrated empirical findings and wisdom from a range of modalities, which should provide some reassurance that you don't just have to take my word for it.

I have also used personal examples to illustrate how I have learned these lessons and put these principles in place in my own life to navigate my personal existential crisis, transition from one career to another, and break up with perfectionism in all facets of my life. Being good has its benefits, but it is not without costs. It is my sincere hope that you find it helpful in stepping out of stuckness, should you find yourself in a situation that is not serving you well.

Afterword

Being good doesn't necessarily mean doing the right thing. In fact, being good can have disastrous consequences. It really depends on the definition and the success metrics you are using for "good". Being good can mean "not causing trouble". This can equate to blind allegiance to a person, belief, or cause that results in harm. Being good can mean "meeting expectations". This can equate to doing what has always been done, without question. Being good can result in perfectionism, people-pleasing, and a puritanical perspective, each in their own way damaging to the individual and those around them.

As a society, we need troublemakers. They are the innovators, the disruptors, the changemakers. Without them, our society fails to evolve; inequality and injustice persist, and entire groups are subjugated. In our personal lives, we may need to cultivate the courage to stop being good and make a change.

That can be terrifying. Especially if we over-identify with the persona of the good girl or boy. For me, my health and well-being depended upon it. Yet, it wasn't my health that gave me the impetus to make a change. I was clinging so tightly to the need to be good and stay in my comfort zone that ticked many boxes of self-imposed expectation, it took a life-altering realisation to get me to release my grip.

When reflecting on the decisions I have made that I have most regretted, almost all of them can be attributed to beliefs I held about the importance of being good and the way that I was defining success in that endeavour. If you accept the premise that all of our decisions are based on either fear or love, all of my regrets were decisions based on fear.

They also share the dubious accolade of being decisions that I intuited were wrong but intellectualised into being right. It took me a long time, and much self-imposed suffering, but I eventually learned the importance of letting go of being good in favour of being kind to myself.

Along the way, I recognised some of the reasons I stayed stuck, and developed some strategies to deal with them. Then I organised those strategies into a framework so I could share it with others, in the hope that I could help them to avoid some of the pitfalls I experienced. Sharing my journey in this book has been one of the most terrifying things I have ever done. I have relived my most difficult experiences, and many emotions have been laid bare.

As I come to the end of this process I have, for the first time in my life, experienced what I believe others have described as cold feet. Except, my experience of cold feet feels like the most intense version of empathic mortification I have ever endured. It feels like hot, anticipatory shame. And it's not some unfortunate tourists I am feeling bad for. It's a future version of myself. One where everyone knows my secrets and thinks I'm pathetic.

My good girl and perfectionist tendencies are in overdrive, and Naggy Nancy has a loudspeaker inside my skull. She is telling me, on repeat, that my book is terrible and that I'm making a

AFTERWORD

big mistake. My body feels almost paralysed, and it is hard to breathe. The temptation to hit delete, rather than send, is strong.

And that is why I am persisting. Because I recognise that if I am still so triggered in this way, after all the work I have done to overcome these fears, my message needs to be shared. It is my sincere hope that this book finds its way to those who need to hear this:

If you are striving to meet the impossible standards of perfection, you can stop doing that now.

YOU ARE GOOD ENOUGH, even when you don't think you are.

Also, shut up, Nancy!

About the Author

Growing up in a small town in regional Queensland, Kate Witteveen always knew she wanted to help others to improve their lives. The eldest child and only daughter of a primary school principal and a primary school teacher, she had a natural affinity for telling people (especially her three younger brothers) what to do. However, despite it seeming like an obvious choice, Kate was determined to chart her own course and do almost anything other than teaching.

After experimenting with a number of university courses and career options, and despite her determination *not* to be a teacher, Kate discovered that teaching may have been in her blood. What started out as sessional tutoring work to supplement her scholarship during her PhD studies, turned into a decade long career in academia. Kate achieved a great sense of satisfaction from teaching and mentoring students, and it seemed as though her career in academia was destined for longevity.

However, as she progressed up the hierarchy at her organisation, Kate found herself being promoted away from what she loved about her job. A perfect storm of organisational upheaval and personal stress brought Kate to a career crossroads in 2018. Despite her love of teaching, Kate decided to leap out of the safety and familiarity of academia, and into the great unknown of business, founding Astute Consulting Services in 2018.

According to the Myers Briggs, Kate is an INFJ. This means she loves people, but not too many of them at once. She is quiet but not necessarily shy. She enjoys real conversations, but small talk makes her uncomfortable. Kate likes to think about things in detail but makes decisions quickly. She loves teaching, but coaching is her passion. She is a recovering perfectionist and is getting better at saying, "no". She falls somewhere between a nerd and an intuit - she appreciates evidence but sometimes knows things without knowing how she knows them. She bemoans the fact that her kids don't seem to appreciate how funny she is, but concedes that is possibly because she laughs at her own jokes before they have had a chance to get them.

In addition to loving all aspects of coaching and training, Kate enjoys relaxing with her husband and three children, running, and curling up with a great book about almost anything. Whilst her favourite genres include historical fiction, personal development, and biographies, she is happy with any book that stimulates interesting conversation or provides new insights. With a personal vision of "excellence through connection," and core values of authenticity, courage, contribution, and wisdom, it is Kate's strongest desire to help others to dream big and live their most fulfilling lives, whilst she aspires to do the same.

Contact details:
kate@astutecs.com.au
www.katewitteveen.com
www.astutecs.com.au

ADDITIONAL RESOURCES AND OPPORTUNITIES

Free Resource

If you would like to reflect more deeply on your own experiences with being good and identify some strategies for exploring other possibilities, download the *Definitive Guide to Breaking up with Being Good* for free:

www.katewitteveen.com

Want to learn more about how you can work with Kate?

If some of the messages from this book have resonated with you, and you would like to learn more about how we can work together, here are some options:

WORKSHOPS AND TRAINING PROGRAMS:

With over ten years' experience in higher education, Kate has established her credentials as an accomplished and entertaining educator. Her style has been described as engaging and easy to understand. Passionate about facilitating quality learning experiences with real-life applicability, Kate is available to present workshops and training programs for organisations and workplaces. For more information, please send me an email: kate@astutecs.com.au

THE PIVOTAL POINT: INDIVIDUAL COACHING PACKAGE

The purpose of this program is to help people who feel as though they are approaching a point in their life when something has to change. You may feel like your well-being is suffering, you are at risk of burning out, you are fed up with feeling stuck, or you want to give perfectionism the flick.

- reclaim your emotional well-being;
- explore your options; and
- create a plan that will enable you to love your life again.

For more information on Kate's offerings and resources, visit:

www.astutecs.com.au

Keen to know what Kate's coaching clients think?

Testimonials

Kate has taught me how to think and how to interrogate my motives and internal self-discouragements. Most importantly, she's shown me how to find my WHY-powers. She's helped me to face and reframe my past, live the now, as well as braving my immediate future. With her help, I'm living a life where I choose to follow my heart instead of my head, where I am okay to develop my own definition of confidence, bravery, and authenticity.

E.L.

Before I met Kate, my life was in chaos. I was completely overwhelmed and heading towards a very dark place. My first session with Kate was life-changing. She helped me clarify the issues, prioritise, develop a plan, and make a start. She is professional yet empathetic, objective but human. She is very good at what she does. My sessions with Kate are invaluable. I cannot recommend her highly enough.

B.M.

Kate is a professional and insightful practitioner, providing confidential individual support to help understand challenges, offering tools and techniques to become the best version of yourself. Kate encouraged me to step out of situations, view them with a wide lens and objectively identify the reason behind it. I now realise the value of a healthy mindset, believing in myself and focusing on what I can control. I accept myself for who I am and can learn from my mistakes, to do better next time and play with possibilities.

M.H.

I find great benefit in talking to Kate. I am a guy who has deployed and found it initially hard to get myself into a room with someone to deal with the ball of stress that I had turned into. After that first session, there was just an extreme sense of calm that you can always return to it with the strategies Kate builds with you. I can highly recommend her services to anyone who needs peace from the inner turmoil.

S.B.

Notes

WHY BEING GOOD CAN BE BAD FOR YOU

NOTES

www.ingramcontent.com/pod-product-compliance
Lightning Source LLC
Chambersburg PA
CBHW021438080526
44588CB00009B/590